The Seven Deadly Virtues

THE SEVEN DEADLY VIRTUES

Eighteen Conservative Writers on Why
the Virtuous Life is Funny as Hell

EDITED BY

JONATHAN
V. LAST

TEMPLETON PRESS

Templeton Press
300 Conshohocken State Road, Suite 500
West Conshohocken, PA 19428
www.templetonpress.org

Designed and typeset by Gopa & Ted2, Inc.

Library of Congress Cataloging-in-Publication Data

The seven deadly virtues : eighteen conservative writers
on why the virtuous life is funny as hell.
    pages cm
ISBN 978-1-59947-460-1 (hardcover : alk. paper) –
ISBN 978-1-59947-461-8 (ebook)   1. Conduct of life–Humor.
2. Virtues–Humor. I. Last, Jonathan V., 1974-
PN6231.C6142S48 2014
818'.602080353–dc23

                                        2014031580

Printed in the United States of America

14 15 16 17 18 19   10 9 8 7 6 5 4 3 2

For Cody, Cordelia, and Emma, who make me laugh

Contents

Acknowledgments

WHEN I WAS fourteen years old, I read Christopher Buckley's first novel, *The White House Mess*, while on vacation at the beach. Some boys watched Neil Armstrong and decided they wanted to become astronauts and go to the moon. I read Buckley and decided that I wanted to move to Washington and become a writer. It never occurred to me that I might become friends with him. It really, *really* never occurred to me that we might one day appear in a book together. Without being maudlin, it is difficult to convey how much it means to me to have Christopher as part of *The Seven Deadly Virtues*. I am deeply grateful.

Not that I'm playing favorites—there are no favorites in our little company. One of the many joys of editing this book was the opportunity to bring together so many of my favorite writers under one banner. Look through the table of contents and what you see is my own private all-star team, the writers whom I look for and admire most. Some of them, like P. J. O'Rourke, Larry Miller, Jonah Goldberg, Mollie Hemingway, and Christine Rosen, I've been friends with for years. Others, such as James Lileks, Rob Long, Joe Queenan, Iowahawk (not his real name), Rita Koganzon, and Michael Graham, I've admired only from afar. Three members of the crew—Andrew Ferguson, Matt Labash, and Christopher Caldwell—have been my colleagues at the *Weekly Standard* for seventeen years, since I was just a kid. They more or less taught me how to write. And then there's Sonny Bunch and Andrew Stiles, whom I've watched grow up and develop into stud writers, too.

I'm thankful to all of them for coming on this joyride.

Mind you, the caper never would have happened if Susan Arellano at Templeton Press hadn't given me the keys to the car and winked, as if to tell me that she probably wouldn't ground us if we brought it back after curfew, even if it had a few scratches on the bumper. And there wouldn't even be a car without the generous support of the John Templeton Foundation and Sir John Templeton. Many, many thanks to them for their forbearance.

Speaking of which, my wife, Shannon, is both my one true love and my editor of first and last resort—an amazing stroke of fortune (for me). I couldn't have done this book—or anything else in life, really—without her.

And the final expression of my gratitude goes to our children, Cody, Cordelia, and Emma, who inspire virtue and vice in roughly equal measure. This book is dedicated to them because, in either mode, they make me laugh. Most of the time.

I love the three of you, all the way to the moon. And back.

—JVL

The Seven Deadly Virtues

Introduction

On Virtues, Past and Present

Jonathan V. Last

A TRUE STORY: The day after I was born, my pediatrician came to the hospital in scenic Camden, New Jersey, to check on me. I was the first kid, and my mother and father were, like most new parents, a hot mess. Into the room strode Dr. Ludwig Schlitt, a German immigrant in his early forties. He was straight out of central casting: trim, ramrod-straight posture; short, clipped hair; and a long face—handsome, in a Teutonic way—that could have been chiseled from the Alps. He bore an uncanny resemblance to the young Christopher Plummer.

Dr. Schlitt poked and prodded and did what doctors do to newborns. When he was satisfied that everything was perfectly *üblich*, he turned to my parents and issued the following verdict/command: "Babies ah a joy. You *vill* enjoy *zis* baby." And with that he turned and strode out of the room, heels clicking on the linoleum as he marched down the hospital hallway.

This is a funny book. You *will* have fun reading this book. Just not yet.

The Seven Deadly Virtues is filled with funny writers. If you want to flip ahead to P. J. O'Rourke or Matt Labash, by all means, go ahead. One of the joys of book reading is that no one makes you eat your spinach first. You can have the ice cream, the pecan pie, the funnel cake, and the chocolate decadence, one after another, and then circle back to the spinach whenever you like. Or even skip it altogether.

But we're going to start with some spinach here, just the same. Because it's good for you. And after all, that's what "virtue" is about.

The Original *Book of Virtues*

In November 1993 an unlikely book appeared at the top of the best-seller lists. Bill Bennett's *Book of Virtues* was a tome; 832 pages of moral instruction. People ate it up. *Newsweek* called it "just what this country needs," and *Time* said it "ought to be distributed, like an owner's manual, to new parents leaving the hospital." Looking at a copy of *The Book of Virtues* today is like examining a relic from some forgotten age. You pick it up, turn it over in your hand a couple times, and think, *People were so different back then. How did they live like that?*

The answer comes in a few different parts. First, it really *was* a different age. Think for a moment about two years—1971 and 1993. In 1971 America was still celebrating having landed a man on the moon. The Watergate break-in wouldn't happen for another year. Vietnam was on a low boil. The Department of Education didn't exist.

By 1993 the Department of Education was an entrenched part of the federal government, and it was the almighty Soviet Union that no longer existed. The Cold War was in the rearview mirror, and with it the space program had begun to wane; an entire generation had never seen a live moon walk, and no American would ever again leave low earth orbit. Instead of looking to the skies, we were looking into screens: The World Wide Web had migrated into common use with the creation of the web browser. The two Americas of 1971 and 1993 were quite different. And here's the kicker: We're as far away from 1993 today as they were from 1971 back then.

Yet some human longings seem innate. The success of *The Book of Virtues* suggested that there was a latent demand for virtue back then, which, at first glance, looks strange from where we sit now. Who would dare suggest today that parents be given a thick book of moral instruction for raising their children? But if you stare hard enough, the picture changes. If anything, we might be more puritanical and values-driven today than we were back then. We just adhere to different values. And boy, howdy, do we cling to them. People still believe in deep moral truths, you see. They simply apply those beliefs in the service of very different virtues.

By the time you read this, the world will have long forgotten Donald Sterling, but the historical record will show that for two straight weeks in April 2014 he was the most important story, and the most reviled man, in America. Sterling was the eighty-year-old owner of a professional basketball team, the Los Angeles Clippers. He had been married to the same woman, a lady named Rochelle, since 1955, but, beginning in 2003, he began carrying on with a series of younger women. And by "carrying on" I mean buying them real estate and cars and bringing them to sit with him, courtside, to watch basketball games featuring the team he co-owned with his wife.

In 2014 the most recent of those girlfriends secretly taped a conversation with Mr. Sterling in which he said some not-very-nice things about African Americans. He used no foul language or racial slurs, but was demeaning and nasty nonetheless. On a scale of 1 to 10, with 1 being your garden-variety bigot and 10 being a KKK Grand Wizard, Sterling was probably a 4. But the tape of that conversation became public, and the great machine that is American society lurched into action, its gears screeching and grinding. Television and radio hosts condemned Sterling; the public convened protests. Corporations that did business with Sterling's team cut ties. The president of the United States—*the president of the United States*—interrupted an overseas trip to castigate Sterling at a press conference. And then the NBA announced that it intended to forcibly terminate Sterling's ownership.

None of this is meant as a defense of Sterling. He seems by all accounts an unpleasant fellow who, more or less, got what he had coming. No, the point is to highlight America's shifting emphasis on different virtues. Sterling's infidelity and the public humiliation of his wife—the woman to whom he had been married for almost sixty years, who had borne him three children—was literally unremarkable. It was mentioned nowhere as a defect of Sterling's character. His private, whispered racist thoughts, however, were important enough to invoke the displeasure of the leader of the free world. They were enough to cause his associates to expel him from their business and deprive him of his property.

In short, think of the litany of shame and approbation heaped on Hester Prynne and then multiply it by a thousand. Except that it wasn't adultery that did Sterling in; it was racism. The scarlet "A" doesn't exist anymore, but the scarlet "R" is very real indeed.

Now, this may well be a positive development. Racism is terrible, and perhaps private racist thoughts are a graver sin than infidelity and the kind of romantic cruelty that causes the breakup of a family. (Rochelle Sterling filed for divorce with improbable quickness.) I'm not a professional philosopher, and this is a safe space. A tree of trust and understanding. A nest of nonjudgmentalism.

But it's clear that the problem *isn't* that we no longer live in an age concerned with virtue. The problem is that we have organized ourselves around the wrong virtues.

The Modern Virtues

Did I say "wrong"? Sorry. That's so judgmental. We're supposed to be in the nest. So let's call them, instead, the "modern" virtues. There are, by my count, seven cardinal modern virtues:

Freedom
Convenience
Progress
Equality
Authenticity
Health
Nonjudgmentalism

If you're going to be one of those uptight philosophical types, some of these virtues are more like values, but I'd argue that this is largely a distinction without much of a difference. These are the characteristics modern society most prizes and has begun to organize its strictures around. Often with nonsensical results.

For example, the writer Mary Eberstadt notes that we live at a bizarre moment when it is nearly impossible to speak with any moral judgment about sexual practices—but a great deal of moral and philosophical energy is spent on the subject of food. You wouldn't dare say that someone ought not put this part there with that person. And you wouldn't say it because (a) your peers would think you a troglodyte and (b) you don't really think it's wrong. It's just a lifestyle choice. Maybe it's not for you, but who are you to judge? Food, on the other hand, is different. It's morally elevated to eat organic grains and eggs that come from cage-free hens. You're a better person if you only eat locally grown produce. A better person, still, if you don't eat meat. And the best people eat with one eye always—always!—on "sustainability." Whatever that is. On the subject of food, some lifestyle choices are better than others. And we're not afraid to say so.

Actually, there is one—and pretty much only one—judgment that you *can* make about sex, and it is this: Imagine that you're in college and one Saturday morning your roommate comes home and proclaims that she just slept with some guy she'd never met and whom she never intended to see again. Could you suggest to her that this might be a suboptimal life choice? Why no, no you could not.

However, imagine that your roommate came home and confessed that she slept with some guy she'd never met and that they had not used "protection." Well, that's a different story. You could lecture her. You could shame her. You could gather your friends and stage an intervention, explaining that this is a terrible, awful thing to do. Downright irresponsible. Something that just isn't done, because you could get a *disease.* Sexual morality is now a function of health outcomes.

And not just sexual morality. Consider smoking. Over the last thirty years, an overwhelming moral consensus has emerged concerning smoking. Where people once smoked on airplanes and in movie theaters and in bars and at home during dinner, today smokers are treated as if they have a terrible and highly contagious disease. They can't smoke in public buildings or often even in public spaces. Smokers are the new lepers, except that no one would look down on a leper as being morally repugnant. Why the reversal? Because it is now universally agreed that smoking is disastrously unhealthy. And healthy living is a cardinal virtue, something to be pursued at all costs, not merely because it is prudent, but because it is good and right.

Yet, at the same time that smoking tobacco has become verboten, smoking marijuana has been gaining wider acceptance. How could this be? It's not like getting stoned is good for you. No, the emerging moral acceptance of marijuana comes when health is trumped by another of the modern virtues—freedom.

Because today we tend to believe that people ought to be able to live however they like, and that societal norms should have little claim on them.

You can see the tensions inherent here. Why should freedom be a virtue when it comes to reefer but not to Lucky Strikes? For that matter, why should health trump freedom in one context but not another? But these tensions aren't unique to the modern virtues. Certainly, the classical virtues are often in tension, too. It can be devilishly hard discerning, for instance, when prudence should override perseverance. Or vice versa.

So, the real problem with the modern virtues isn't that they're contradictory—the classical virtues can be just as confused. And it isn't that they're somehow "wrong" as virtues. Equality, authenticity, a devotion to physical health, and even nonjudgmentalism can be fine things, taken in right measure. No, the modern virtues fail because, for the most part, they concern the outer self, the human façade, the part of ourselves that the world sees most readily—while the classical virtues form an organizing framework for our inner selves . . . for our souls, if you believe in that sort of thing. And it turns out that when you scale people out to the societal level, the superficial moral framework of the modern virtues turns out to be an insufficient organizing principle. When it comes to virtue, the old ways are still the best ways.

The Perils of Virtue

If you're looking for a good explanation of the old ways, you could do worse than Alasdair MacIntyre's summation of Aristotle. Here's MacIntyre explaining what virtue really is:

> The virtues are precisely those qualities the possession of which will enable an individual to achieve *eudaimonia* and the lack of which will frustrate his

movement toward that *telos*. . . . For what constitutes the good for man is a complete human life lived at its best, and the exercise of the virtues is a necessary and central part of such a life, not a mere preparatory exercise to secure such a life. . . . Virtues are dispositions not only to act in particular ways, but also to feel in particular ways.

There's a lot to unpack in those ninety-four words, even if you remembered what *eudaimonia* is. (Don't worry, I didn't either.) But overall, it's a fine working definition of virtue: Virtues are the internal qualities that allow us to be our best selves and enable us to lead complete and fulfilling lives. When you think about virtue in that sense, you really understand why the modern virtues are so inadequate. Being your *authentic* self and living a physically *healthy* life are clearly second-order goods. To be your best self and live the most fulfilling life, it's far more important to exhibit, say, charity and courage.

Yet one of the recurring themes you'll find in the pages to come is that extremism in pursuit of virtue can easily become vice. Which is to say, no single virtue is, on its own, necessarily virtuous. Hope is essential for the human spirit, yet when it stands alone it turns its bearer into a Pollyanna. Charity—one of the greatest of the virtues—is sublime, yet if you have nothing but charity, you might well become gullible. Curiosity is wonderful; without it we'd still be living in caves and clubbing large animals with sticks. But curiosity run amok, and unleavened by other virtues, turns you into a gossip. Or worse. Mengele was a curious sort.

I don't mean to be overly dramatic, but history is full of monsters created by manias for a single virtue. Robespierre, for instance, was devoted to justice. When he fostered the Terror it wasn't an accidental by-product of his wild pursuit of virtue—it was his object: "Terror is naught but prompt, severe, inflexible justice," he wrote. "It is therefore an emanation of virtue." Yikes.

If you take anything from this book (other than the yucks), it should be that virtue is additive. No single virtue is sufficient in and of itself, and each one, taken on its own, is corruptible. Yet each virtue becomes more valuable with the addition of others. And for any single virtue to be brought to its full bloom, it must be surrounded by its sisters. Courage and prudence: Together they give people the spine to do great things. Integrity and forbearance: Without them, no society can function. Chastity and temperance: All right, let's not get carried away here. The point is, when a man has cultivated the virtues as a class, then, and only then, does he become a man in full.

Of course, not everyone can be expected to cultivate all of the virtues at all times—we are not, all of us, Augustines. We have to muddle through as best we can and pick our spots. So how do we keep our imperfect devotions to virtue from becoming malformed? In Patrick O'Brian's *Master and Commander* books, Stephen Maturin, a physician, philosopher, and spy, notes that virtue should always be commingled with humor. This observation is, I think, the best engine governor we have for virtue, to keep it from pushing the needle across the line and into the red zone. I'd bet just about anything that Robespierre never laughed about justice.

The Heavyweight Championship of Virtues

All that philosophical stuff is nice enough, but this is America, where we love winners. So what you're probably thinking right about now is: *Fine, no single virtue is good enough on its own. But which virtue is the best? Who's the king of the virtues?*

Picking a favorite virtue is like picking a favorite child: It's the kind of thing you're supposed to pretend not to do—but that everyone does anyway. We can toss chastity and temperance out of the ring straight off, obviously. They're important, in their way, but exactly no one is going to make them contenders for the title. Same for thrift and simplicity. Nice to have, but not first-tier virtues. Fellowship is fine, but a luxury. And justice? As Rob Long suggests some pages down the line, that's the virtue we'd much rather have done unto others than practiced on ourselves. No thanks.

Some pages after that, Christopher Caldwell argues a pride of place for curiosity, "because the knowledge acquired through curiosity grounds your other virtues, while leaving to you the choice of what those virtues will be." Aquinas called prudence the queen of the virtues, saying that she gently guides all the rest. And Aristotle deemed courage to be the first virtue, because it makes all the others possible.

Good points, all of them. And you probably have your own favorite. But I'd like to make the case for gratitude. Cicero declared, "Gratitude is not only the greatest of virtues, but the parent of all others." It is the alpha, the point from which all virtues must begin. It is gratitude that allows us to appreciate what is good, to discern what should be defended and cultivated.

You need not believe in God to pursue the virtues (though it certainly helps). Yet if you do believe, then your first instinct in all things must be gratitude: for creation, for love, for mercy. And even if you don't believe, you must start again from gratitude: That a world grown from randomness could have turned out so fortuitously, with such liberality. That the Hobbesian state of nature has been conquered. At least for a spell. As my friend Yuval Levin explained not long ago, "We value these things not because they are triumphant and invincible but because they are precious and vulnerable, because they weren't fated to happen, and they're not certain to survive. They need us—and our gratitude for them should move us to defend them and to build on them."

Gratitude magnifies the sweet parts of life and diminishes the painful ones. It is the wellspring of both humility and ambition, the magnetic pole for prudence, the platform for courage, the inducement to charity and mercy. And in addition to everything else, gratitude is the engine for progress: We build not because we are dissatisfied with the world as it is, but because we are grateful to all those who have built it to this point and wish to repay them by making our own contributions to their work.

None of this is to say that the world is perfect—it isn't. But if it's to be improved, that improvement will come one person at a time, through the exercise of virtue—through the conscious decision of all of us to try to be better people, to live better lives, and to make a better world. All of which begins, from first light, with saying "Thank you" for what we have, right now.

Which is where I'll start: Thank you for picking up this book and spending time with me and my friends.

And that's all for the spinach. Now go and have some fun.

Part I

The Cardinal Virtues

The ones you were taught in Sunday school
but have totally forgotten about until this very moment.
Go ahead. Try to name them.
We'll wait. . . .

CHAPTER 1

The Seven Deadly Virtues
And the New York Times

P. J. O'Rourke

BEFORE WE CONSIDER what virtue has been up to lately, we should take a look at how vice is faring.

The conceit of every era is that people are more inclined to vice than they used to be. In *The Clouds*, first performed in 423 BC, Aristophanes has the personification of "Just Discourse" recount how vicious children are nowadays, compared to the youngsters of yore who "would not have dared, before those older than themselves, to have taken a radish, an aniseed, or a leaf of parsley, and much less eat fish or thrushes or cross their legs."

What Aristophanes said is true to this day. I've seen a child, sprung from my own loins, munch a radish. With crossed legs. And before I've even mixed a predinner martini. (Although, in fairness to our kids, we have trouble getting them to eat fish at all, or aniseed, or parsley—never mind thrushes. Their penchant for vice does not extend to calling first dibs on gobbling roast songbirds.)

The long-lost "Golden Age"—a time when people and things once were better—is a myth in every mythos. I'm willing to bet that Australopithecus shamed its biped brats with stories of noble hominids brandishing proper tails and blissfully living in trees.

That said, vice is doing very well these days. Note, for example, how practically everything featured in the *New York Times* Sunday Styles section is one of the seven deadly sins.

For starters, envy might as well be the section's title. There's not a person in the Styles section who isn't leading a life that's more celebrated, glamorous, rich, exciting, dramatic—or, at the least, more stylish—than our own. Every advertisement is a promotion of avarice. You could, I suppose, be charitable (charity *is* one of the seven virtues) and believe that the baubles being hawked are all meant to be given away as gifts to the poor—a Coach bag for the bag lady, a Montblanc pen for a homeless man to letter "Will Work 4 Food" on a piece of cardboard. But even if that were the case, a remarkable degree of avarice would have had to be practiced by the givers in order to afford such gifts in the first place. As for pride? Pride goeth before a *New York Times* wedding announcement.

Fashion, of course, is the handmaiden (excuse me, handperson) of lust. You might not think that, given some of the fashions you see in the *Times*. But then again, everything according to taste. The presentation of purple hindquarters excites the mandrill. And who am I to presume that *Times* readers are less sensuous than this noble primate? Then there's the sloth evident in just having enough time on your hands to bother reading the Styles section. But whatever else you want to say about the Styles section, you can't accuse it of gluttony. The people you see pictured are always beautiful and terribly thin. No, for gluttony you have to go over to the paper's "Dining Out" section. The portions may be small, but the prices are voracious. And as for wrath, well, just consult the *Times* editorial page. Or consult me after I've read it.

So vice flourishes. Does virtue languish in its shade? Gol durn right, it does, I say, stopping myself just short of committing the mortal sin of taking the Lord's name in vain. Not to mention committing the unforgivable sin against the Holy Ghost—*despair*.

I mean, who even remembers the names of the seven virtues these days? Well, except justice. That gets a lot of play. But as for the others . . . I've never seen protestors marching through the street shouting, "No justice! No prudence!" Here, for the record, is the list:

1. Prudence
2. Justice
3. Fortitude
4. Temperance
5. Faith
6. Hope
7. Charity

These are the so-called Seven Cardinal Virtues. Although, technically, if you possess Virtue #5–Christian Division, only the first four are cardinal, so called because they were the principal virtues handed down from the ancient Greek philosophers. The last three—faith, hope, and charity—are theological virtues, supplied by the New Testament because the ancient Greek philosophers were hopeless logic-choppers who detested each other and had faith in things like a nature deity with a goat's bottom who played a wooden kazoo.

Not that there haven't been competing lists. The fourth-century Christian poet Aurelius Clemens Prudentius composed a different roster of "Seven Heavenly Virtues" in *Psychomachia*. (It was a medieval best seller.) Prudentius, despite his cardinal virtue of a last name, chose chastity, temperance, charity, diligence, patience, kindness, and humility.

People will have their own partialities, of course. For my own part, I'm not so sure about diligence. It depends on what you're being diligent about. There is the kind of hollow, due diligence that JPMorgan Chase did on Bernie Madoff's transactions. Or, for those who like their moral turpitude without fear of an SEC investigation, there's the abhorrent manner in which a grown man "diligently" learns to master *Grand Theft Auto V*. But note that "self-esteem" doesn't make anybody's list.

Virtues are hard to tabulate because being good is an inversion of Tolstoy's maxim about families. Indecencies are all alike; every decency is decent in its own way.

And *inversion* is just the word for virtue's current state. Virtue has by no means disappeared. It's as much in public view as ever. But it's been strung up by the heels. Virtue is upside down. Virtue is uncomfortable. Virtue looks ridiculous. All the change and the house keys are falling out of virtue's pants pockets.

1. *Prudence* has become such an object of scorn that a call to violate it is the motto of the world's most famous sneaker company. (Perhaps you ought to think it over for five seconds first. "Just do it" ranks second only to "Watch this" on the list of phrases most commonly heard before gruesome accidents.)

People will name their children anything these days. Anything. It wouldn't surprise me to find out there are half a dozen boys in my son's fourth-grade class named Aurelius. But there's no girl named Prudence in any grade school in America, even though "Dear Prudence" was a Beatles song that sucked—which is usually enough to send American parents into a nomenclature frenzy. (See the half-dozen boys in my son's class named Jude.)

Why is prudence so unpopular? Because it's become synonymous with an unhealthy inhibition resulting in psychologically damaging exclusionary behavior toward those with a healthy *lack* of inhibitions. How accepted is the shaming of prudence? These days, no politician, pundit, celebrity, public intellectual, mainstream Protestant minister, or Reform rabbi can rebuke *any* type of personal behavior without the disclaimer, "I'm no prude, but. . . ."

That is, unless the personal behavior in question can be construed as exclusionary, racist, sexist, homophobic, insensitive, exploitative, or right-wing extremist. In which case no prudence will be exercised in branding the person whose personal behavior is in question as one or more of the above. The majority of voters in "red states" are also fair game.

But the truth is, prudence is the first of the virtues. You can't name one good thing that's been done that couldn't have been done better with more prudence. (Except for my wife marrying me.)

2. *Justice* is justly sought. But justice is also what everybody claims he wants but nobody seems happy about when he gets it. It's the "Aw-I-don't-want-anything-for-Christmas" present of virtues. And it's the one virtue that's better when we practice it on others than when others practice it on us. As a priest friend of mine says, "I don't know about you, but on Judgment Day I'm going to be praying for mercy, not justice."

3. *Fortitude* is quaint. We praise the greatest generation for having it, but they had aluminum siding, church on Sunday, and jobs that required them to wear neckties or nylons (but never at the same time). We don't want those either. Instead of fortitude we seek help from others. There's nothing unvirtuous about that. But when help isn't forthcoming, fortitude is what we used to need. Now we need to complain. The lionheart has been replaced by the caterwaul: "She's so brave to be talking about this." Instead of holding onto our courage, we share our fears. Lacking prudence, we prize impulsiveness. And sharing is such a generous impulse.

4. *Temperance* has become a twelve-step program. We praise it unstintingly, thirty days a month, while we're at Promises in Mailbu. For the rest of the year, well . . . temperance doesn't

make good reality TV. Or garner YouTube hits for celebrities. And temperate political speech is an easy way to lose a political primary.

I'm no prude, but . . . as described in the *Catechism*, temperance "ensures the will's mastery over instinct and keeps desire within the limits of what is honorable." Yet mastery is nowadays unacceptable in the home and the workplace, at school, and anywhere else except among consenting adults in one of those West Village dungeons you see profiled in the *Times* Sunday Styles section every so often. And as for the rest of what the *Catechism* says about temperance? Instincts are good things. Desires must be fulfilled. And "limits of what is honorable"? That's so judgmental.

5. *Faith*, however, should not be tempered. Or should it? There's such a thing as a surplus of faith, and we've got it. Faith in ourselves is an article of faith, and we have the utmost faith in the businesses and industries devoted to this faith—psychiatry, psychology, therapy, counseling, self-help books, and motivational speakers.

We have faith in man and all his works (unless they have a large carbon footprint). And all his empty promises, too. Indeed, the more empty the promise—free health care!—the more faith we seem to have in it. So, for instance, a Yale University website says 70 percent of Americans have faith that the climate is changing. As well they might, since a sign has been given unto them. The climate changes every year, getting warmer in the spring and colder in the fall. And of course we have faith in all sorts of things we see on the Internet.

We have faith in government, although we may deny it thrice before the cock crows—and more often than that after a couple of drinks. But the very size of the Leviathan is a mark of our faith. The U.S. government dwarfs the Cathedral of Saint John the Divine or any megachurch. Tithing? Government lays claim to 40 percent of our entire GDP. And, as for government services, daily attendance by Americans is almost 100 percent. Church is just once a week, and less than one-third of us go that often.

There is one sort of faith that's on the wane in America. More than one-third of us aren't certain about the existence of God—or say we don't know, or don't believe in Him at all. At least that's according to the Pew Research Center, in whose polls we have faith.

6. *Hope* . . . and change! That pretty much tells us where this virtue has gone—down the rabbit hole of wishful thinking. Hope was not always so faint a word in the English language. The root meaning is "expectation of a thing desired." In the *Book of Common Prayer* during "The Order for Burial of the Dead," the presiding minister says, "the sure and certain hope of the Resurrection." He doesn't mean, "Wouldn't it be nice if . . . ?"

But hope has been out of artistic fashion for more than a century. It's hard to think of a great modern novel, play, or poem that ends on a hopeful note. Or even begins on one. Take the first line of "The Waste Land," for instance: "April is the cruelest month." Excuse me, Thomas Stearns, Mr. soon-to-be Anglican convert, did the Easter Bunny skip the Eliot household? *The Great Gatsby* concludes with F. Scott Fitzgerald declaring, "So we beat on, boats against the current, borne back ceaselessly into the past." And smack into the dock, no doubt. Even when he was a lad taking sailing lessons, there was no hope for Scotty.

True, the last words of dialogue in Henry Miller's *Death of a Salesman* are from Willy Loman's wife, who says, "We're free . . . . We're free. . . ." But Miller isn't proposing an ontological truth in order to refute determinism. He's just being fashionably ironic. What Linda Loman is talking about is how the final mortgage payment on the house was made the day of Willy's funeral.

If you judge by the number of apocalyptic movies released

lately, there's no hope in popular culture either. Somebody's probably working on an end-of-the-world remake of *The Sound of Music.*

> DOE, endangered species deer
> RAY, the earth collides with sun
> ME, the only person left
> FAR, Zombies! I'd better run
> SO, what am I going to do?
> LA, the town this crap comes from
> TEE, been there, got the shirt too
> Which brings teens back to see . . .

Movies like this over and over again.

7. Charity, however, we do not lack. As long as it's tax deductible.

Or go to any wedding. No matter how godless is the couple, the groomsmen, the bridesmaids, or for that matter the officiant, you'll be forced to endure a bowdlerized version of 1 Corinthians 13 that goes something like this:

> Though I speak with the tongues of men and angels, and have not Amnesty International, I am become as sounding brass. PETA suffereth long, and is kind; Doctors Without Borders envieth not; the Sierra Club vaunteth not itself, is not puffed up. Planned Parenthood is not easily provoked, thinketh no evil; UNICEF beareth all things, believeth all things, endureth all things. And now abideth Nature Conservancy, Make-A-Wish Foundation, Habitat for Humanity, these three; but the greatest of these is United Way.

Of course, usually the Revised Standard Version of the Bible is used, with the word "love" in place of "charity." They're not the same thing. In Greek (which was the language of Saint Paul in his letters to the Greeks in Corinth) there are four words for love. *Eros* is love in almost the only way we talk about "love" anymore except (let us invoke the virtue of hope) when we say we love our children. In that case, we mean *storge*, or affection. "I love you, dude," is *philia*, or friendship. The word Saint Paul uses, however, is *agape*, the unconditional love of God and all his creation. Invoking the virtues of hope *and* faith, let's suppose that's what they're doing at the United Way.

Which points to the nonprofit nature of practicing the virtues in the modern world. Virtue survives. It just doesn't provide modern Americans with the minimum compensation that they feel is necessary to meet their basic needs.

Prudence keeps you out of the stock market. Justice costs like heck in legal bills. Fortitude is expensive, what with the cost of mixed drinks these days. Temperance, ditto, what with the cost of Promises in Malibu. Faith is broke—broken when the Democrats caved in on a budget deal that didn't extend unemployment benefits. He who dines on hope is sure to lose weight. And charity begins at home. This is why you're still living in your mother's basement.

The wages of sin may be death, but the wages of virtue are $7.25 per hour. Unless Congress changes the law.

CHAPTER 2

Prudence
Long Live the Queen

Andrew Ferguson

PRUDENCE IS an intellectual virtue, the moral theologians tell us, sometimes even called the "queen of the virtues." Without its power to humble and restrain, many other virtues collapse. This shouldn't be news to us. We live in a time when prudence often goes missing, taking lots of things with it.

The lack of prudence breeds a kind of silliness that only very sophisticated people are capable of; certain forms of ignorance are available exclusively to intellectuals who know so much that they have forgotten how much they don't know. Into this category—which is really very crowded, and getting more crowded by the day—I place an evolutionary psychologist named Satoshi Kanazawa.

Kanazawa's field, evolutionary psychology, is part of what has been tagged the New Science, the application of the methodologies of the physical sciences to realms of human behavior— our motives, habits, morality, emotions, instincts, likes, and dislikes—that had until recently been considered beyond the reach of clinical experiment and computation. Once upon a time, we understood our social and interior lives through philosophy, religion, art, poetry, music, mythology, storytelling— all the wellsprings of humanism. Now we forage in such fields as "sociobiology," "behavioral economics," "social psychology," "neuroeconomics," "cognitive sociology," even "experimental philosophy," to plumb the deepest truths about ourselves.

Kanazawa is a popularizer and booster of this New Science, as well as a practitioner. A professor at the London School of Economics, widely published in professional journals, he has for several years written a column, "The Scientific Fundamentalist," for *Psychology Today*. The column carried a motto of his own choosing: "A Look at the Hard Truths about Human Nature." Note these are *hard* truths he deals in. Like so many New Scientists, Kanazawa considers himself a wake-up-and-smell-the-coffee guy: a man bringing news of unavoidable, sometimes unpleasant, facts. He's proud to say he's willing to look reality in the eye. Unlike some people. You know who you are.

In early 2011 Kanazawa devoted a column to one hard truth that nobody had dared to point out before—indeed, a hard truth that nobody had even suspected was true. Kanazawa alone had been brave enough to make the necessary scientific inquiry.

"Women on average are more physically attractive than men," he announced. This, it should be said, is kind of true, though it's truer to say that in many surveys women as well as men tend to rate pictures of women more highly than pictures of men.

"So women of all races," Kanazawa went on, "are more physically attractive than the 'average' . . . *except for black women.*" The italics are his. In case readers failed to catch on, the editors of *Psychology Today* provided a helpfully question-begging headline: "Why are African American women less physically attractive than other women?"

Being a good evolutionary psychologist, Kanazawa festooned his column with multicolored graphs and packed it with elaborate descriptions of his methodology. He had reached his remarkable conclusion, he revealed, by using a dataset from Add Health, a government-sponsored survey that interviewed adolescents over a period of years as they passed into adult-hood. Among other things, interviewers rated the kids on their physical attractiveness.

"I can compute the latent 'physical attractiveness factor' by using a statistical procedure called factor analysis," he wrote. "The latent physical attractiveness factor has a mean of 0 and a standard deviation of 1." Latent factors, statistical procedures, standard deviations . . . what could be more authoritative? The scientist allowed himself discursive asides: "It is very interest-ing to note that, even though black women are objectively less attractive than other women, black women and men subjec-tively consider themselves to be more physically attractive." Very interesting indeed, Herr Doctor! And of course he pro-posed an evolutionary theory to account for the hard truth to which his factor analysis led him. It sounded terribly scientific, it really did: "The race *differences in the level of testosterone* can potentially explain why black women are less physically attrac-tive than women of other races." This time the italics are mine.

Now, a few characteristics immediately leap out at any reader unlucky enough to happen upon Kanazawa's piece. First among them is this: It is the work of a man unconstrained by prudence of any kind—intellectual, moral, social. There is the grandi-osity, his unexamined confidence that the truths of human behavior can be captured in numbers and under controlled conditions. And there is the obvious methodological flaw: He uses subjective rankings by anonymous questioners of unidenti-fied research subjects as a proxy for large, objective facts about entire classes of people. There is his pose as a disinterested observer, shrugging on his lab coat and pretending to follow the data wherever it leads him. And above all there is his reduc-tionism, as though the conclusion he's drawn about a made-up "physical attractiveness factor" could scarcely be otherwise thanks to the chemical composition of the human body, as it has been brought to us by natural selection.

In one sense, of course, Kanazawa is an extreme case. *Psychology Today's* editors dropped him as a columnist after more than sixty of his fellow evolutionary psychologists published an outraged letter insisting that Kanazawa "does not represent evolutionary psychology." And this was also true, in a small way. Evolutionary psychology is one of the most fashionable of the disciplines in the New Science, and as a rule it attracts only the most careful careerists. None of them would be capable of the indiscretion that goosed Kanazawa into publishing a "finding" that (he must have known) most readers would find not only ludicrous but offensive.

But that demonstrates a lack of prudence in the most superficial sense. On a deeper level, Kanazawa represents the New Science very well; he is in fact an exemplar. The reductionism, the dubious methodology, the touching faith in numbers: They all indicate a profound lack of intellectual modesty. Boorishness, the very opposite of prudence, is the hallmark of the New Science.

We should be careful to distinguish the New Science from the physical sciences, which it resembles only in pantomime. The astonishing success of the physical sciences, from molecular biology to astrophysics, is what gives the New Scientists the confidence to pretend they're doing the same thing the big boys are doing. The confidence, as we'll see, is badly misplaced. Experiments that furnish the data for the New Science lack the test tubes, the microscopes, the particle accelerators that so impress us laymen about traditional science. Because the New Science takes as its subject such hard-to-pin-down phenomena as thoughts, motives, mental impressions, emotional reactions, and so on, its data are rather more elusive, too.

Most often the data are generated straight from the classrooms and psych labs of major universities. Commonly, a varying number of undergraduates are asked by graduate students or their professors to pretend they are in one artificial situation or another, take tests about their reaction to the made-up situations, and then collect a modest sum of money or course credit for their trouble. At an apparently higher level of rigor—but not really—the students do the same thing while magnetic resonance images are made, resulting in colorful pictures of brains lighting up like Clark Griswold's Christmas tree. The data yielded by these or other implausible methods are tortured by statistical analysis into the equations and charts and graphs that crowd the impenetrable prose of the published paper.

And then, at last, comes the insight into how and why humans do what they do. Let's consider some findings of the New Science—all of them breathlessly reported by a gullible media with lots of airtime and massive editorial holes to fill. No phrase in modern journalism is so overused as "studies show," unless it's "research reveals" or "experts say."

As a general rule, the findings of the New Science fall into one of two categories: They are trivial when true, and untrue when not trivial. One would have thought that Aristotle, for instance, had pretty much nailed the subject of happiness. He spent a whole book in his *Ethics* thinking about it! But now the old Greek egghead has been outdone. In Berkeley, California, the university's Greater Good Science Center employs researchers in, yes, happiness studies. Specialists have engaged undergraduates in countless role-playing experiments. (At Berkeley, samples of undergraduates are disproportionately white or Asian, female, and unusually brainy, but they are taken as representative of humanity in general.)

Through role-playing, the happy scientists have discovered

that delaying gratification may lead to higher levels of oxytocin than simply satisfying desires as they arise. Oxytocin is a little reward cooked up through natural selection to make us happy. The ever-ready MRI machines have discovered that performing acts of kindness "lights up the left prefrontal cortex." Other surveys of undergraduates tell us that a group performing various tasks skillfully provokes more favorable chemical reactions in their frontal lobes than a group that performs the same tasks poorly.

So now we know, thanks to the New Science, that if you want to be happy, you should delay gratification, be kind to others, and manage your affairs competently. It's science. Who knew?

Well, down the ages, lots of people knew this—and they discovered it without access to psych majors or MRIs. But to the ear tuned to twenty-first-century buzz-buzz, the truisms of common sense and tradition sound much more authoritative if they're preceded by the magic words "Studies show. . . ."

A pile of studies in the New Science has been rising on my desk over the last few months. All of them are certified by scientists at top universities. Here we go:

An online survey of 334 subjects shows that parents accidentally confuse children's names more often when the names of the children sound alike. MRIs from Western University in Ontario show that students well-trained in arithmetic are "better equipped to score higher on PSAT math." Economic researchers "applied a Two Stage Least Squares methodology" to a set of real estate listings and discovered that "unattractive real estate agents achieve quicker sales." A pair of evolutionary psychologists at Bristol University studied the "beer goggle effect"—the reputed tendency of men to find less attractive women more appealing after a few drinks—and discovered that it had evolutionary roots. (In the New Science everything must have evolutionary roots.) It seems that our earliest ancestors learned to value symmetry in facial composition because it is a signal of a healthy reproductive capacity; in time we humans took to calling this "beautiful." Alcohol blurs our genetically controlled ability to judge symmetry, hence the beer goggle effect. Katy, bar the door!

It's tough to choose a favorite from my stack, but I'll do it anyway: It relates to the evolutionary psychology dogma that men prefer a woman who has a waist-to-hip ratio (WHR) of 0.7. According to standard New Science method, this preference has been taken to be a universal impulse bred into our prehistoric ancestors and survives today as an evolutionary adaptation. Now, as it happens, the preference is not universal; men in China seem to favor a WHR of 0.8, for instance. Such an inconvenient fact does not deter the march of evolutionary psychology, however, because its practitioners have already come up with a theory to account for the universally preferred ratio.

So what's behind the WHR? Women with a 0.7 ratio very often have higher levels of estrogen, indicating fertility and general good health. Evolution thus favored men who favored these women, and a universal fact of human nature, a conception of beauty, was bred into our genes. This is an excellent example of New Science reasoning. Strained logic arises from a shaky factual basis to reach a conclusion that is simply an extension of the premise: Evolutionary psychology assumes that all basic human behavioral traits are adaptive, and therefore the WHR preference must have been adaptive.

But there's more! To confirm the theory about WHR, two evolutionary psychologists at Maryhurst College came up with another experiment: If the WHR theory is true, then stressful circumstances, which make men less inclined to reproduce, should alter their preference to a less estrogen-friendly ratio. On went the lab coats, out came the spreadsheets, and the two

researchers gathered up every cover of *Playboy* magazine from
1960 to 2000. Yes, they really did. And they discovered that in
periods of economic recession, the WHR of the bunnies on the
cover rose from the standard 0.7. In times of stress, men liked
heavier women, according to the Bunnies. QED, as the Romans
used to say; "research reveals," as we say.

Such reasoning brings us the "fat gene," "the morality mole-
cule," "the infidelity neuron," and all of the other discoveries
that parade across the pages of *Time* and *Psychology Today* and
the stage sets of *Today* and *Good Morning America*. A neuro-
surgeon at UCLA has even discovered the "Jennifer Aniston
neuron," which controls a man's reaction to the aging starlet.
Jealous colleagues are now in pursuit of the Julia Roberts neuron and the Halle Berry neuron. You think I'm kidding? The
New Science would indeed be merely comical—the credulity of
smart people is endlessly amusing—but for two considerations.

First, our infatuation with a reductionist, materialist conception of life has real-world effects, in marketing, business organization, even public policy. Some of the effects are more serious
than others. A few years ago, interior decorators across Europe
and America began painting corporate headquarters and work
spaces green after researchers "discovered" that green was the
color most conducive to creativity. (The evolutionary explanation: On the prehistoric savannah, our ancestors learned to
associate green with water, nutrition, plant life, and, of course,
fertility.) The painters had to be called in again' after a year or
two, when other researchers (working on a different group of
undergraduates, no doubt) found that exposure to the color
blue "can double your creative output." (The new evolutionary
explanation: Our cleverest ancestors were stimulated by the
cerulean sky, the azure sea. . . .)

But more ominously, the New Science is invading government, too. "Behavioral economics," whose practitioners swal-
low the findings of social psychology without a second thought,
is now the guiding principle of much economic policymaking.
There is no reason why this should be so. Behavioral economists were as clueless as old-fashioned economists, for example,
in failing to foresee the financial collapse of 2008, the single
most calamitous economic event of the past eighty years. Nev-
ertheless, President Obama called in the behaviorists when it
came time to design his "middle-class tax cut" in 2009. It was
supposed to goose consumer spending, and hence economic
growth.

The tax cut was an exercise in "framing." New Scientists
are mad for "framing." They believe (studies show) that how
an object, idea, or event is presented, described, or packaged
determines how people will react to it. With the tax cut the
question was how the money should be placed in taxpayers'
hands. A lump-sum "tax rebate" in 2001 had failed to stimulate
the economy (research revealed). But if the tax cut were made
slowly—by changing the rate of withholding in workers' pay-
checks—then they would be more likely to spend it.

How did our behavioralists "know" this? Well, once upon a
time, graduate students at Texas A&M assembled 141 undergraduates and asked them to pretend they were going to be
given sums of money in either monthly or annual increments.
Two-thirds of the group were women, all were young, some had
business experience, others didn't. Not exactly a cross section
of America, much less of humanity—but so what? This is science. So the kids filled out a questionnaire. And what do you
know? The ones who had been told they would be paid annu-
ally said they thought they wouldn't spend the money as readily
as the kids who were told they'd get their money monthly.

And so a tax cut created by the government of the almighty
United States of America was "framed." Taxpayers saw small

increases in every paycheck, just as the data had dictated. And then . . . nothing happened. The economy remained stuck. Per capita spending didn't increase. The incremental framing was no more successful than the lump-sum "bonus" had been. What went wrong? Well, the behavioralists had failed to consider other truths that the data didn't show—commonsense truths, human truths that lay beyond the grasp of their questionnaires. For example, 200 million taxpayers in the grip of a recession react differently from college kids doing a thought experiment in a classroom at Texas A&M. Perhaps in hard times, citizens are more likely to save an increase in their resources than spend it, no matter how the matter is "framed." Or maybe this whole "framing" thing is simple-minded.

Every now and then, as the New Science continues to roll through every area of American life, from baseball to fashion design, we see signs of intellectual prudence resurfacing, evidence here and there of a restraining modesty—the caution and second thoughts that true prudence requires of thinking people. Critics of evolutionary psychology are publicly making the case that our knowledge of prehistoric life is inevitably too sketchy to use as a basis for psychological speculation about contemporary life. A small but noisy number of social psychologists have begun to point out the shoddy experimental practices common to their field: small sample sizes, a failure to replicate findings, a misuse of statistical protocols. People are increasingly aware that some of its most cherished findings— which have subsequently been built into countless other studies as operating assumptions—cannot be confirmed. These admirable science cops have even deployed humor and parody to make their point. One impish researcher, for instance, undertook to prove that time travel is real, and succeeded.

His experiment demonstrated, through the application of an accepted but impenetrable methodology, that listening to a certain Beatles song could reduce an undergraduate's age by one year. Now we have to change the song's title to "When I'm Sixty-Three."

Yet the heedless march continues. I said awhile back that there were two considerations (you forgot already?) that made it hard to dismiss the imprudence of the New Science as merely comical. The first is the practical influence it has over intellectually unarmed laymen like management consultants, television producers, science reporters, marketing professors, and the writers and readers of pop science books. The second consideration cuts deeper.

We live in a post-Christian age. Or so we're told. The metaphysical assumptions that once served human beings in understanding themselves and their relationship to the world are no longer accepted, certainly not by our most educated and admired thinkers. So now is as good a time as any to quote G. K. Chesterton's great aphorism: When a man ceases to believe in God, the danger isn't that he will believe in nothing, but that he will believe in anything. Into the vacuum left by the traditional view of a man—a unique being created by God, endowed with a soul, infinitely precious—comes the thin and desiccated conception that is both the premise and conclusion of the New Science: A human being is a member of a not-so-special species, tugged and pulled by unconscious impulses, the random consequence of a blind and pointless process stretching back to the beginning of time.

No one actually believes this, of course; a person who truly lived by the New Science metaphysics of humans as soulless robots wouldn't be a skeptic, he'd be a psychotic, unconstrained by the most elemental assumptions that make us civilized. Virtues can be cultivated, said the ancients, but they are also innate. Maybe they're an evolutionary adaptation.

It turns out that prudence is harder to shake than we might have thought. In our daily lives, as we struggle to get along with each other, some form of prudence retains its hold over us; it is there to tame the wild thought, stay the impulsive hand. It is a mystery beyond the reach of science, old or new. Lucky for us, we still live in a world where prudence, as often as not, remains enthroned as the queen of the virtues.

CHAPTER 3

Justice
The One Virtue Nobody Really Wants

Rob Long

TWO WEEKENDS AGO, on a Saturday afternoon, I made a tragic and irreversible mistake.

I went to Costco.

Which is not, of course, a mistake in general. Big warehouse stores are great places to find roast chickens, gallon drums of mayonnaise, and batteries sold by the crate. At my local Costco, I can guide a small, boat-sized trolley through the aisles and fill up on enough garbage bags, pinto beans, and multivitamins to last the calendar year. I love Costco so much, I often find myself yearning for the (inevitable, for Los Angeles) 7.0 earthquake— the Big One—just so I can finally make a dent in my enormous stockpiles of Ramen noodles and baby wipes.

The problem is, on a Saturday afternoon, everyone else is doing the same thing. The spaciousness of the store and its radiating vibe of plenty are ruined by all of the other people banging into you with their giant carts, or crowding around the pallet of vacuum-sealed ribs, or creating long, snakelike lines at the register.

On this particular Saturday, somehow, it was worse. The place was so packed, I couldn't even make it to the aisle where they keep the drums of ketchup.

What did I do to deserve this? I asked myself, as I threaded through the masses. *I guess in a previous life I must have burned down an orphanage.* That's one way of looking at the idea of justice: It's payback for your sins. In a previous incarnation, I suppose, I was one of those evil warlords who marauded through the Steppes. No, being a warlord is hard work, even for a previous-life version of me. Maybe I was a Dickensian villain who hated orphans ("Those big eyes! Those smudgy faces! Are there no workhouses?") and I did something truly evil—I burned down the orphanage, orphans and all!—and now the universe was getting its revenge by making me wait thirty minutes to check out of Costco.

Payback received.

Justice, in this view, would be more like the ancient Vedic idea of karma—that balancing force of nature that connects everyone to everything (and vice versa) and punishes wrongdoing in ripples that radiate through many lifetimes. It's an irritating philosophy, obviously, because I'm almost entirely certain that any previous lives I may have had—and, for the record, I didn't have any—weren't spent marauding, but rather cowering in a hut somewhere wet and cold or, at the very most, kneeling submissively before some psychopathic ruler while blubbering out ridiculous and desperate flattery. I mean, that's basically what I do in *this* lifetime. (I work in Hollywood.)

In other words, what did I do to deserve this throng at the local Costco? And the short answer is: nothing. So if the Costco debacle was karma, then it was unfair. Unjust. All I did, really, was sleep a little too late on a Saturday morning to beat the crowds.

When seen that way, as a series of tiny, needling pinpricks—sleeping an extra hour gets you punished with a crowded warehouse store—then the exotic, incense-heavy notion of karma starts to look a little less spooky and grand. It's not capital-J Justice. It's *karmic* justice. It's justice lite. And the punishment of karmic justice isn't meted out over the decades and lifetimes. It happens in the here and now, probably within some sort of twenty-four-hour statute of limitations. When you get right down to it, karma isn't such a big and complicated idea at all, which is probably why they talk about it so much in yoga class.

What's attractive about karma, though, is that it's automatic. Karma is an invisible balancing machine that's always running in the background. Karma just happens. Justice, on the other hand, needs a push.

That's why we say we're "bringing" someone or something "to justice." And you never, ever, say, "We're bringing that guy to karma."

In the Asian subcontinent, where karma was invented (or discovered, depending on how you view these things), the climate is often so inhospitable that it's no wonder people developed a vaguely *mañana* attitude about these kinds of things. It's stifling hot or raining monsoons, and there are stinging insects all over the place. You can practically hear them saying, ages ago, during the era of the Upanishads, "Let's just let karma get that guy, okay?" Someone's using a banana-leaf fan and they're sitting in the hot shade and he's all, "I am *not* bringing anyone to anything in this weather."

Move a little to the west, and the culture develops a more hurry-up kind of urgency. Colder weather, perhaps, clarifies the mind. And so karma gets a little goose and the idea of "justice" takes hold. Justice is karma on a timetable. Justice is what karma becomes when a bunch of Type-A dudes get hold of it.

The problem is, justice is complicated, with lots of moving parts and a terrifying margin of error. Justice is something people do *to* other people, and if there's one thing we've learned from history, it's that most things people do to other people aren't very nice. Even when—maybe *especially* when—they're driven by good intentions.

"Your Honor, I have a problem," the prospective juror said to the judge during jury selection a year or so ago. The prospective juror—just so you don't get the wrong idea—was not me.

I'm a good citizen and a patriot, and I believe in the process—messy and flawed—of justice. So when I get a summons to appear for jury service in Los Angeles County, I obey it. (I postpone it several times, of course, and then whine about it constantly, but I *do* eventually show up.) I have a wide and expressive face, one that radiates a kind of sunny fairness—you're just going to have to take my word for that—and so I almost always make it to the jury box for the voir dire process. I usually last until I announce my occupation—I work as a television writer and producer in the entertainment industry—at which point the defense attorney thinks to himself, *This guy is a pampered plutocrat who hates minorities and the underclass,* and the prosecutor thinks, *This guy is a guilty white liberal who thinks all defendants are innocent.* And I end up excused for another two years. (Ironically, both lawyers are essentially correct.)

Last year, though, I made it through a couple of rounds. The prospective juror to my left—female, thirtysomething, expensive watch, Kate Spade tote—squirmed nervously as it became clear that the jury selection process was winding to a close and that she was going to be on the panel. So she raised her hand in a desperate gambit to get out.

"Your Honor, I have a problem."

Her problem, she told the judge, was that the defendant in the trial—it was an assault case, and a pretty serious one—had come to court in his prison jumpsuit. He was surrounded by people in suits and court uniforms and here he was, the unfortunate, in a costume that screamed "Guilty!"

"How can I be impartial when I keep seeing him in that outfit, like he's already guilty?" she asked.

The judge explained, carefully, that each defendant in the hot and dusty county of Los Angeles has the right to appear in court wearing pretty much whatever. The defendant could have worn a suit. He could have worn a scuba outfit. He *chose*, probably on the advice of counsel, to wear his orange prison overalls.

"But why would he do that?" she asked.

"Well," the judge said carefully, "that's what we're going to find out during the trial, right? What his story is."

She shook her head. "I just can't see him impartially," she said. "Not in that outfit."

The judge looked annoyed. "Justice, ma'am," he said, pointing to the Great Seal of the Los Angeles County Courts, with a depiction of Lady Justice, the Greek goddess Themis, who holds up the scales with her eyes blindfolded, "is blind."

"Yeah," she said. "But I'm not."

And with that, she was excused from jury service. "Nice one," I whispered to her as she shuffled past me. She shot me a dirty look.

Justice may be blind, but we aren't. We are very much sighted. We see the assault-and-battery defendant in the orange jumpsuit. We see the insider trading defendant in the $530 Brioni T-shirt. We notice when class and status get dragged in irons to the dock, and it's hard not to think, *Okay, maybe he's innocent of that specific charge, but the guy is clearly a bastard. He's guilty. Of something, anyway.* We may have a goddess as a symbol, but justice is a human sport.

Interestingly, the supernatural world doesn't need a system of justice. Vampires, for all of their seductive power, can't really bend the rules: The sun comes up and they die. Shoot a werewolf with a silver bullet and that's that. No litigation necessary, or even possible. It's only humans, with their endless capacity to whine and beg and wheedle and wiggle out of commitments, who need an institutional mechanism for justice and law enforcement. Everyone and everything else just sucks it up.

During the economic meltdown of 2007–2009, when the financial bubble inflated by mortgage-backed securities collapsed in a pile of bank failings and taxpayer-supported bailouts, some financial masterminds suggested a unique way to reform the financial oversight bureaucracy: Abolish most of the financial institution regulatory mechanisms and replace them with a simple agreement.

Take the top 5 percent of the employees of any bank or financial institution that does business in the United States and make them pledge 99.9 percent of their net worth toward any future settlement or bailout that the federal government (i.e., the American taxpayer) is obliged to cough up in case of their failure.

The bailout would naturally exceed the amounts collected, of course, but it would be fun to see high-flying investment bank vice presidents tooling around town in Hyundais and Kias rather than BMWs and Bentleys. It would be immensely satisfying to watch the 1 percent trade summers on Nantucket for summers around the backyard above-ground pool, in a neighborhood without a Whole Foods or really good sushi.

Would it compensate the taxpayers? Oh no. Not by a long shot. But boy, would it hurt the investment bankers. And maybe that's enough.

The idea behind the proposal, though, was that the automatic karmic punishment would be so unthinkably painful—"Tristan? Sophie? I have some bad news. Tristan, you're not going back to Andover next year, you're going to George Washington Carver High. Sophie, you can't take that unpaid internship, you're going to work at Quiznos with baggies on your hands"—that it would create its own kind of powerful regulatory oversight. Don't want to slip down the class ladder?

Then maybe you'd better run the numbers again on that risk-blind derivative of a Class-B tranche of mortgage-backed securities you've just option-swapped.

We're supposed to be talking about *justice*, of course. Yet why is it that we always seem to end up talking about *punishment?*

For the record, the defendant in the orange jumpsuit was clearly guilty. He didn't really contest the issue in the ensuing trial, which I couldn't evade. What he wanted, it seemed, was to be seen as someone who had already served some time in prison—hence the strategic choice of wardrobe—in order to appeal for leniency. Which he didn't get. When we talked about it in the jury room—and here, I hope, I'm not breaking the law—there was lots of talk about "time served," but also lots of talk about "sending a message" and "getting tough" and "making sure the punishment fits the crime."

It turns out that a randomly assembled group of Los Angeles County voters—minus the subset of thirtysomething females with Kate Spade totes—can't exactly be Blind Justice Holding the Scales, but they can, in a disorganized and rambling way, get to the point and come up with a reasonable, though imperfect, way of dealing with a defendant in an orange jumpsuit who beat up his girlfriend.

I held that last detail back, did you notice? And did you also notice that the minute you read that final clause—"beat up his girlfriend"—the whole story seemed different? Justice may be blind, but we're not.

When you know what he did, you want to throw the book at him. For something, anyway. When you know how he assaulted his girlfriend—and, as jurors, we knew; we saw the emergency-room photographs, which were catch-your-breath shocking—you're not going to let him walk. You're going to bring him to justice, even if he'd already served some time, even if he was "deeply committed to anger-management counseling," according to his lawyer. Even if he had already lost his job and (in a detail that was never explained to us) his car as well.

What we talked about in the jury room, then, wasn't really justice. It wasn't guilt or innocence. In most trials, that's already pretty much decided. No, what we balanced, not so blindly, was punishment. We didn't discuss the fairness of the process or social inequality or the state of the public schools or cultural differences. We talked punishment, as in, if we find him guilty of this or that charge, in this or that degree, what's the guy going to get? To the extent that a jury has an ability to influence or shape the punishment, that's what we focused on.

Not justice, really, but whether this guy would get punished harshly enough to deter him from doing this again, but not so harshly that he never gets out from under the cloud of the conviction. The scales of justice, which are supposed to balance the evidence of guilt or innocence, really end up balancing something more personal and human: revenge and mercy.

Well, maybe "revenge" isn't quite right. (Though it's not quite wrong, either.) When business pundits and L.A. jurors sit around trying to sort things out, it's hard for them to totally ignore the devil on their shoulders urging them to *make this guy pay.* Justice is something people do to other people, often with a vengeance. It's measured not in time served or fines paid but in the sting of the punishment, the pain of the sentence. Justice—to be truly satisfying—has to hurt.

Which is why, I think, justice is something we prefer to mete out rather than to receive. And why, I think, the groovy, loosey-goosey, super-chill vibe of karma is so appealing. *It's the universe, man.* Not a bunch of harried and preoccupied strangers in a drab jury room trying to sort out big issues.

But the universe has no appeals process. You can't ask karma for a second chance. You can't explain yourself to the cosmic balancing system and ask for a little wiggle room. You sleep late on a Saturday and Costco is going to be *hell*.

What we're all looking for—even as we devise more draconian and painful punishments for our fellow man—is a little mercy. Justice we've got. Justice comes in great floods and firestorms over Sodom and Gomorrah and fifteen-to-twenty with no parole. Justice—and even low-calorie karma—can seem awfully cruel, even when it's about as fair and dispassionate as possible.

It's not hard, then, to see how the simple message of a Jewish carpenter in Nazareth became so popular. Jesus didn't talk much about justice. He talked about mercy. He talked about forgiveness. As his followers see it, Jesus is the Chief Justice of the Court of Appeals, Universal Circuit. And he's a pretty lenient jurist.

There are constellations of theology going on here, with tangles of writings and memoirs and lives of the saints spanning two thousand years of debate about God's mercy tempered with his justice. But when you hear a gospel group sing "Jesus Dropped the Charges," it all kind of clicks into place.

"I was guilty," they sing, "Of all the charges":

> doomed and disgraced,
> but Jesus,
> with His special love,
> saved me by His grace;
> He pleaded
> And He pleaded
> He pleaded my case.
> Jesus dropped the charges,
> Jesus dropped the charges,
> At Calvary I heard Him say,

At Calvary I heard Him say,
At Calvary I heard Him say,
case dismissed, case dismissed. . . .

It may be hokey, but it's also a lot truer than most things we pretend to think about justice and fairness. We're not really looking for balanced scales or blindness. Oh, yes, maybe that's what we think is right for the other guy, but what we really want to hear—when we spend a night totaling up our transgressions and petty actions and lies large and small—is forgiveness. To hear "case dismissed." To walk out of the courtroom of life a free man, touched not by justice but by mercy.

To sleep as late as we like and glide though a near-empty Costco.

CHAPTER 4

Courage

The Rise of "Shelter in Place" America

Michael Graham

IN 1965 CIVIL RIGHTS activist John Lewis helped lead six hundred marchers across the Edmund Pettus Bridge in Selma, Alabama, walking headlong into the violence of fire hoses, tear gas, and stick-wielding state police. Lewis was twenty-five at the time. He got his skull fractured for his trouble. Yet despite repeated attacks, arrests, and trips to jail, Lewis continued to lead civil rights protests across the South and was eventually elected to Congress from the once-segregated state of Georgia.

That was then.

In 2013 someone spray-painted the phrase "Knights Don't Need No Ni**as" on the home of a mixed-race high school student in Lunenburg, Massachusetts. (The Knights were the mascot of the football team, for which the kid played.) There were no fire hoses. No dogs. Just a splash of spray paint. The response? The family immediately pulled their son out of the school. And then the school cancelled the entire remainder of the football season. Just *cancelled* it.

Asked why he took such drastic action in the face of a single act of intimidation, the Lunenburg High principal responded, "I thought, 'Would I bring my own kids to a game?' And the answer is 'No.' Why? Because it wasn't safe to play." A suburban high school football game wasn't . . . "safe"? What did he think was going to happen? That the Aryan Nation Air Force would drop KKK paratroopers onto the field?

While heroic school officials waged a brave battle against "Mississippi Burning: Massachusetts Edition," over on the West Coast another great American was calling on his inner Braveheart in an epic struggle to the death. With his house pet.

In early 2014, Lee Palmer of Portland, Oregon, got upset when his cat, Lex, scratched his seven-month-old baby. He gave the twenty-pound Lex a good kick in its backside. The cat, according to Palmer, suddenly "went off over the edge." It began running around the room, hissing and spitting. Palmer and his baby mama, Theresa Barker, grabbed the baby—and their *dog*—rushed into the nearby bedroom, and slammed the door. Every time they opened it, the ferocious feline greeted them with a growl.

Being modern Americans, they did what comes naturally when confronted with terror. They called 911. Here follows— hand to God—the actual transcript of the call:

PALMER: He's very, very, very, very hostile. . . . He's charging at us! He's at our door. . . . Did you hear him scream?

CAT: Raaaaaarrrr!

"It's easy to laugh," Ms. Barker solemnly told reporters afterward. "When this happens to you, I assure you, you will do the same thing." We have to laugh, lady. To keep from *cringing*. When you have a grown man afraid of his own housecat, you've moved beyond mere cowardice. When you have a suburban school official too scared to face Friday Night Lights, you've abandoned the very idea of courage. And so we have. The descendants of Sam Adams and Paul Revere, who ran to the sound of the guns so that they could face the most deadly army on the planet, have devolved into "shelter in place" Americans who cannot bear even the sight of a gun, much less the sound.

It gets worse. In 2011 more than forty members of the Burlington, Massachusetts, police department—including a SWAT team and a crew flying a helicopter—rushed to the local mall because a woman reported seeing a man "with a short rifle" roaming the hall outside Banana Republic. The mall was quarantined. The nearby interstate was shut down. Hours later an employee at a nearby medical office who walked through the mall from the bus station every morning saw the news on TV. He started to wonder if the umbrella sticking out of his backpack that morning might have sparked the alarm.

At first he dismissed the idea, because (a) it's an umbrella, and (b) he had seen the usual security guards hanging out that morning and not one of them had approached him. But being a good citizen, he called the cops anyway and, sure enough. . . .

There was a time when, if a panicky granny started talking about seeing rifles in the food court, a security guard would have checked it out himself. Then—in the wildly unlikely event someone with a gun *was* planning target practice at Target—he would have called the cops. This would have been about the same time in our national history when the police, getting a report of an alleged gun sighting by a single, wobbly witness, would have sent a squad car to investigate. And again, if it had been the one-in-a-million "mall terror" moment, he would have called for backup. Instead, the old biddy made her report, the mall cops called the real cops, and the coppers responded by sending in a small army with tactical weapons and air support.

Why didn't common sense win the day? Because everyone involved was too scared. After the debacle had been sorted out, the security guards claimed that they considered it their job not to *find* the rumored rifle, but to run away from it. They called the cops and hid. And the Burlington police chief publicly *praised* them for doing just that—right before he defended his decision to spend tens of thousands of dollars and tie up the interstate over an umbrella. In fact, the chief went so far as to say, "I would hope that if the exact same thing happened tomorrow, they [the panicked witness and first responders] would do the same thing."

The moral of the story isn't that this one police chief is ridiculous. It's that his attitude is now our societal default: Any risk is seen as an unacceptable amount of risk.

In the land of red, white, and blue, yellow is the new black.

How did a nation born in rebellion become a place where we let the government tell us what size sodas to drink? Why are we willing to suffer the human cattle call of airport security, with grown men sullenly standing in their stocking feet, wingtips in hand, while the lady in front of them gets groped by handsy TSA agents?

It's not because we live in a more dangerous world than our eighteenth-century ancestors did. Far from it. Setting aside the horror of 9/11, we Americans have never been safer, healthier, or more secure. Violent crime rates have collapsed. In a nation with more than 300 million people, we average just over one hundred abductions by strangers each year. The death rate for car accidents is way down. Even our fireworks—the last bastion of socially sanctioned physical recklessness—are safer. Seriously. More people were killed in 2009 by vending machines falling on them than were sent to their maker by recreational explosives.

But watch the news—or talk to your neighbors—and you'll see a society living as though mortal danger lurks around every well-lit corner. We have to show ID in order to enter worksites that have never been safer. We keep our kids off sidewalks and out of parks that have never been more secure. As a nation, the world's greatest military and economic superpower peeks out across the horizon like an elderly lady behind her lace curtains, nervously eying the neighborhood teens smoking by the lamppost.

What's going on is that Americans have embraced a cowardly moral calculus: Do something, and if it doesn't work out you'll get blamed. Do nothing, and maybe no one will notice. Every few months there's a story about someone in distress—a lost child, a sick senior citizen, a hit-and-run victim lying in the street—and how long it took for a Samaritan to stop and help. "I wanted to stop but I was afraid." "What if I got sued?" "What if I got in trouble?"

Americans in past generations dealt with these same worries, too, whenever they rushed to the aid of strangers or stepped in to defend a woman's honor. But they were also haunted by other questions—namely, "What would people say if they found out I did nothing?"

Back then, the fears competing against our courage were counterbalanced by the power of shame. Not anymore. Because when everyone shelters in place, then no one has to feel guilty about it.

Everything about the phrase "shelter in place" irks my inner American. I hate the bogus sense of action being slapped onto this pseudo-gerund. "Shelter" is a noun, and trying to turn it into a verb, like "efforting" and "journaling" is a con on the body politic.

No one said "shelter in place" when I was growing up. So far as I can tell, the first usage in the media dates back to 1987, when it was used to describe the safety protocol for a chemical plant malfunction. In fact, the term was almost entirely confined to that one area—industrial chemical disasters—throughout the whole of the 1990s.

No, I never encountered this icon of cultural cravenness—which is now standard operating procedure—until the Boston Marathon bombing in 2013. In the aftermath—which included a shootout with the terrorist Tsarnaev brothers on the streets of Cambridge—local cops launched a manhunt for the younger brother, Dzhokhar. The teen, injured but on the run, was a terrorist, for sure. But he wasn't a Tom Clancy–style supervillain. He was an evil nineteen-year-old idiot who needed to get rounded up by the posse. Yet as the cops, the feds, and every agent of the government short of SEAL Team Six searched for him, the governor gave the order for residents of the greater metropolitan Boston area—all four million of us, spread out over fourteen hundred square miles—to "shelter in place." Stay home from work, skip school, hit pause on your daily lives. All because of the fear aroused by one wounded, backpack-toting teenager.

And we—the residents of the cradle of the revolution—*complied.* The Minutemen shot. We "sheltered."

The shelter impulse starts early. Parents buy their toddlers "Thudguards"—helmets they're supposed to wear while learning how to walk. We're not talking about biking or skateboarding—this is protection from the dangers of *toddling.* Once the citizen-infant has mastered the hazards of bipedalism, we promptly order them to stop: No walking to the park, or to the corner store, or to a friend's house. Because it's a dangerous world out there.

We don't even let our kids walk to school. In the 1960s, about half of American schoolchildren were walkers. Today the number is around 10 percent. And the folks who do let their kids walk? May God have mercy on their souls. In 2009, a Mississippi mom named Lori Pierce let her ten-year-old walk to soccer practice, about a mile from their home. "Several people who saw the boy walking alone called 911," the *New York Times* reported. "A police officer stopped him, drove him the rest of the way and then reprimanded Mrs. Pierce. According to local news reports, the officer told Mrs. Pierce that if anything untoward had happened to the boy, she could have been charged with child endangerment." (Take a moment to appreciate that a boy walking to soccer practice in Mississippi was so scandalous that it made the *New York Times*.)

Once the kid gets to school, it's not a lot better. Surely you've heard about "zero-tolerance" policies: The six-year-old boy in Colorado kicked out of school for violating the "sexual harassment" policy? (He kissed a little girl.) The elementary-school student in Arkansas taken into police custody for pointing a chicken nugget at a teacher and saying, "Pow pow"? It's evident to anyone paying attention that zero tolerance equals 100 percent stupidity. But you have to understand that zero-tolerance rules aren't about protecting kids. They exist to protect the adults who are too cowardly to make judgments.

Consider: Two kids bring a knife to school. One is a hood wannabe with a serious knife; the other is an honor student with a pseudo-spork to cut her lunchtime apple. In a culture with a dollop of courage, one student would be in serious trouble and the other would either be ignored or gently reminded to leave her spork home next time. And then, when parents showed up at school demanding to know why Sluggo was treated differently than little Sally, the administrator would explain that there are real and material differences between the cases, and by the by, they might want to lock it down at home before Sluggo is initiated into MS-13.

But that would involve courage. So instead we teach our kids that there's no difference between totin' a gat and biting a toaster strudel into an L-shape that vaguely resembles a gun. (Yes, a kid was really punished for making a "Pop-Tart pistol." I told you we're scared to even look at guns.)

We continue this adversity avoidance through high school and often into college. Then we wonder why "adult" college grads flock home to Mom and Dad to sleep under their Transformers bedspread and sign up for health care on their parents' insurance.

Courage—the notion that resolve in the face of difficulties and strife is a good thing—has withered before our eyes. And it's dying because we have smothered its food source: adversity. There can be no courage without fear. There can be no bravery without danger. This is the nonnegotiable proposition every person and society face. And as a nation, America looked at this deal and said—*We'll take it!* If living in a land without risk means a culture without courage, we have no problem with that.

Except that there is a problem. Adversity cannot be banned. It falls from the skies in hurricanes, tornadoes, and ice storms. It pounds greedily on our door when it thinks we're unprepared and the police are unavailable. It flies in on airplanes, with evil plans and box cutters. It is always—*always*—floating about, ready to interrupt normal life at a moment's notice.

Affluent suburbanites may believe courage is passé, that

they've achieved real security by living in good neighborhoods and installing home security systems. They think they have barricaded their lives forcefully enough to keep danger forever at bay. Most of the time, they're right—but every once in a while they're wrong. Anyone who dies fat, happy, and unafraid in their beds without ever having faced a moment of danger has done so not through careful planning but sheer, dumb luck.

Most of us won't be that lucky. More importantly, most of our children won't either. One day, they will turn and find danger staring them in the face. And whether it's the darkness of human nature or the mindless violence of Mother Nature, they're going to need courage to bear it.

Will they have that strength? Will they even understand the danger when it finds them, or will they desperately pound the screens of their iPhone demanding "Where's the app for this?"

America isn't, won't be, and shouldn't be Sparta. We don't need parents abandoning middle schoolers in the wilderness with a pocketknife and a compass and saying, "If you're not home by Friday we're renting out your room." But we should give up the notion that danger and discomfort are, in and of themselves, bad things—signs that someone has done something wrong, that some policy must be changed . . . that danger can, through careful planning and lots of bureaucracy, be eliminated. This notion couldn't be more wrong.

If you're a parent, and you're sending away to college kids who've never been asked to do a task that was too hard, or been given a responsibility they didn't believe they could bear, or have never been asked to suffer a single moment for the sake of another—you haven't succeeded. You've *failed.*

Courage is the essential virtue. What good is intelligence, if you're not strong enough to stand up for good ideas? What's the point of moral understanding if you lack the guts to do the right thing? What help is love if you don't have the heart to defend those precious to you? Without courage, then prudence, wisdom, charity—every virtue on the list—all come to naught.

Most of us will never have to run to the sound of guns. But let's not, at least, run from the sound of cats. Instead of trying to banish adversity, we ought to welcome at least some of it. Because it can make us a more courageous—and better—people.

CHAPTER 5

Temperance
The Deadliest Virtue

Andrew Stiles

WE'VE COME A LONG WAY since Prohibition, which, as everyone now knows, was the greatest blunder in American history not directly attributable to Jimmy Carter. Like so many other human miseries, the ban on alcohol is now mostly confined to pockets of the developing world, and is unlikely to make a comeback in industrialized societies anytime soon. That's a good thing. If countries such as Libya, Sudan, and Yemen hope to one day reopen the debate by demonstrating the societal benefits of being high and dry, they have a long, hard slog ahead of them. And we shall fight them every step of the way.

What's so virtuous about temperance? The late Christopher Hitchens, whose atheism ran as deep as his love of the sauce, observed that Jesus's transmutation of water into wine was "the only worthwhile miracle in the New Testament . . . a tribute to the persistence of Hellenism in an otherwise austere Judea." Well? Is he wrong? As Tex Ritter—admittedly a lesser, more contemporary prophet—once sang:

> Beefsteak when I'm hungry
> Rye whiskey when I'm dry
> Greenbacks when I'm hard up
> Religion when I die

Note the sequence. Because like it or not, that's the world we've living in. Temperance almost always takes a back seat to more enjoyable proclivities. Those who preach it are written off as squares and scolds, doomed to inhabit that most deplorable station, on the "wrong side of history."

We're living in an age where a high-functioning alcoholic (and recreational crack smoker) can become the mayor of the biggest city in Canada and, well, just keep on being mayor like it's the most natural thing in the world. Rather than being cast off as a moral destitute, Toronto's Rob Ford became a cartoonish antihero who could win the Internet just by showing up at McDonald's at three in the morning and babbling in a Jamaican accent.

Temperance took a back seat in Brazil, site of the 2014 World Cup, where a decades-old law prohibiting the consumption of alcohol at soccer stadiums—passed because the country led the world in stadium fatalities—was discarded under pressure from the sport's governing body, FIFA, and the tournament's chief sponsor, Budweiser. And why not? Better to go out in a drunken riot than to subject yourself to ninety scoreless minutes of "the beautiful game" while stone sober.

In spite of all this, civilization is doing just fine, thanks. The demise of Prohibition has not, as the squares foretold, brought about the end times. Granted, it spawned three or four generations of degenerate buffoons. And yes, our universities are more likely to be fonts of binge drinking and underachievement than of scholarship and human flourishing. But there are plenty of celebrities who aren't in rehab, and it's not like *all* of our major cities are run by charismatic, quasi-functioning drunks. So sure, there have been some downsides to letting the booze flow. But all in all, it's been a relatively small price to pay. Because the benefits of living in a less temperate society are splendiferous.

In 1830 an Amherst professor named Edward Hitchcock penned an essay urging the "young men of America" to abstain from alcohol, which, in his assessment, tended to "weaken the memory, unfix the attention, and confuse all mental operations." Which, of course, is very much the point of alcohol.

We've all made the mistake, for example, of not cracking open a bottle of an intemperate substance before asking our aged uncle how his drive up from Florida was—and being forced to listen as he describes every lane change, rest stop, and highway exit in excruciating detail, including the various weather patterns he encountered on the way.

Booze can help you deal with these sorts of crises. It is a great emancipator, freeing us from our obligation to suffer through tedious conversations with some of society's most difficult personalities—not just relatives, but also hipsters, vegetarians, marathon buffs, and soccer fans. And more often than not, it also frees us of the burden of appearing interesting and charismatic. Simply laugh out loud at every joke, buy a round for the table, and people are bound to accept you as a normal human being. We drown life's inanities in a sea of drink. It's for our own good.

Professor Hitchcock was particularly concerned that "intemperance seems to select the brightest intellects as her victims, that she may show her omnipotence by crushing them in her iron embrace." It was imperative, he wrote, that abstinence be taken up by "literary men." He wasn't joking.

It's a shame Chris Hitchens is no longer around to give us his thoughts on the subject while making his way through a bottle of Johnny Walker Black. Being the bright intellect and literary man he was, Hitchens understood as well as anyone that copious drinking was not only a "professional deformation" among the literary class, but in many cases a professional prerequisite.

This is especially true of political writers, such as myself. Imagine having to start your day at a nine o'clock Congressional hearing on ermine subsidies without a flask, or, in dire situations, a CamelBak. Or sitting in front of your computer that afternoon, trying to write about the hearing and make it sound interesting without a tumbler in your desk drawer. Or worse: Imagine trying to endure the endless parade of Washington "networking" events—full of former class presidents, policy nerds, and sweaty interns handing out business cards—without an open bar. Oh, the humanity.

The truth is, our nation's capital would cease to function in the absence of free-flowing spirits, a fact not lost on the people who run this town. In February 2013, "investigators" from the District's Office of Weights & Measures carried out a series of raids on bars and restaurants along the rapidly gentrifying H Street Corridor, a popular destination for the millennial hordes who swim in the slipstream of, and in many cases run, the great Leviathan. Armed with beakers and graduated cylinders, the crew of government employees spent "about an hour and a half measuring our drinks and pitchers," an astonished restaurant owner told the *Washington Post*.

Their objective was not to curtail the flow of hooch, but rather to enforce the legal requirements governing the appropriate volumes of beer, wine, and liquor in response to citizen complaints that they were "not receiving advertised amounts of alcohol." Temperance be damned: The capital of the free world will not abide its citizens getting drunk at a rate slower than the law provides. A century ago, the jackboots came to pour your whiskey out in the street. These days, they top up your glass. That's change we can believe in.

It would be premature, however, to write temperance out of the history books just yet. Regrettably, the would-be prohibitionists have become increasingly emboldened. Modern-day temperance mongers are waging new, targeted offensives on more favorable ground—and occasionally winning. Former New York City mayor Michael Bloomberg is their patron saint; the man rarely met something he didn't want to ban in the name of the public good. While in office, the courageous billionaire successfully outlawed a variety of petty scourges such as trans fats, salty foods, large sodas, Styrofoam packaging, and overly loud headphones.

Cigarettes, too, although that goes without saying. Mayor Bloomberg was hardly the only public official to crack down on cancer sticks. Smokers nationwide have been relegated to specially designated areas, forced to huddle like refugees in quarantine. (That's not an entirely bad thing, insofar as getting drunk in New York bars is now slightly more enjoyable for nonsmokers.) Now, everyone agrees that cigarettes are bad for you. If you smoke, you shouldn't. And there's a whole industry designed to help people quit with products like the e-cigarette, which mimics the act of smoking by producing a nicotine-infused water vapor.

You might be thinking: That sounds like a great idea with very little downside! Well, see, this is why you can't be trusted. In one of his final acts, Mayor Bloomberg banned these too, on the grounds that they might cause some people to *start* smoking real cigarettes. Was there any science behind this concern? No. But that never stops the temperance nannies. They know what's good for you, and if you don't like it you can go to the designated smoking area and light up your coffin nail with the other lepers. At least, until they bulldoze the designated smoking area and put in a bike share.

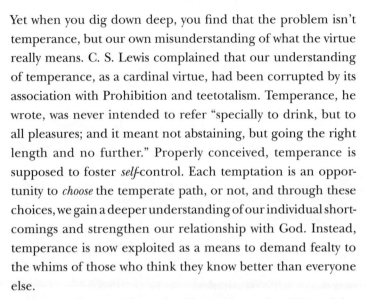

Yet when you dig down deep, you find that the problem isn't temperance, but our own misunderstanding of what the virtue really means. C. S. Lewis complained that our understanding of temperance, as a cardinal virtue, had been corrupted by its association with Prohibition and teetotalism. Temperance, he wrote, was never intended to refer "specially to drink, but to all pleasures; and it meant not abstaining, but going the right length and no further." Properly conceived, temperance is supposed to foster *self*-control. Each temptation is an opportunity to *choose* the temperate path, or not, and through these choices, we gain a deeper understanding of our individual shortcomings and strengthen our relationship with God. Instead, temperance is now exploited as a means to demand fealty to the whims of those who think they know better than everyone else.

Lewis understood how obnoxious this can be. "One of the marks of a certain type of bad man is that he cannot give up a thing himself without wanting everyone else to give it up," he wrote. The whole point "is that he is abstaining, for a good reason, from something which he does not condemn and which he likes to see other people enjoying." Man is free to give up "all sorts of things for special reasons—marriage, or meat, or beer, or the cinema; but the moment he starts saying the things are bad in themselves, or looking down his nose at other people who do use them, he has taken the wrong turning."

Martin Amis may be less convinced than Lewis as to the merits of a virtuous lifestyle, but he has respect for temperance, too: "It all comes down to choices, doesn't it? . . . Do you want to feel good at night or do you want to feel good in the morning? It's the same with life. Do you want to feel good young or do you want to feel good old? One or the other, not both."

As long we're free to make those choices, temperance is

actually quite important. And if we're going to try to sell temperance to modern America, we might make use of another idea that's in short supply: shame.

Shame might be the best way to nudge members of the millennial generation—whose everyday conservations are often a discourse on the question "How drunk was I last night?"—into embracing a more temperate lifestyle. The Department of Defense, for example, actually runs a sort of temperance program aimed at young members of the U.S. military, warning them not to develop a reputation as "That Guy." The message is fairly straightforward: Make good choices, and don't make an ass of yourself.

Sound advice. Because in the digital age, our most intemperate acts can be easily recorded and uploaded to YouTube. A pulsing hangover can be the least of your problems after an overnight bender—just ask David Hasselhoff or Alec Baldwin. In a world where reputations can be scuttled in an evening, shame can, and should, help instill in us an understanding that not every story that begins with "This one time I was so drunk . . ." is a story worth telling.

Because at some point, those stories become increasingly hard to top. If your night out doesn't end with you waking up in a Russian mobster's penthouse, chained to a radiator, while a midget wearing chaps pours champagne over your recently shaved head, then you're just not down with YOLO, bro. Eventually, even Hitchens found virtue in temperance, warning us young folks that hangovers were a "bad sign," that blacking out was "an even worse sign," and that neither should be cause for celebration. And the older we get, the truer that becomes.

The best case for temperance I'll ever see was demonstrated by a fellow I knew in college named "Larry." (Not his real name.)

He quickly became known as "The Dude," for his somewhat excessive efforts to imitate—in both personality and physical appearance—Jeff Bridges's character in *The Big Lebowski*. Larry was uncoordinated, and suffered from poor balance whilst sober, which he rarely was. He carried an enormous key chain that would clank and chime like a set of prison cuffs everywhere he went. You could hear him coming a hundred yards away. You could hear him fall from twice that distance, like a felled bison exploding a jukebox. After a string of minor incidents, he wound up in the hospital one night after being bested by a set of stairs and a few too many pints of Jamesons.

When he emerged several days later sporting a thick bandage on his forehead, he informed us that the injury was severe enough as to require a skin graft, which had been taken from a fleshy portion of his posterior. He had, quite literally, made an ass of himself.

Temperance may not be the most popular of virtues. But it is also, occasionally, essential.

CHAPTER 6

Hope

Chicago Is a Place Called Hope

David Burge (aka Iowahawk)

THERE'S A RAMSHACKLE STADIUM on the corner of Addison and Clark in Chicago that houses an (ostensibly) professional baseball team. As of this writing, that team has managed to complete 105 seasons of play without a World Series title to show for it. One hundred and five seasons. During that stretch, twenty-one other baseball franchises have celebrated a world championship. This list of winners includes multiple titles for every extant 1908 American and National League club (the Braves won championships in three different cities), not to mention the likes of the Florida Marlins, a franchise that is as ridiculous as it sounds and that, by the way, didn't even exist until the Cubs' drought was in its eighty-fifth year.

The sheer statistical improbability of this streak is somewhat astonishing: My back-of-the-spreadsheet calculation says it's about 0.004, or a 250-to-1 shot. Had you been a prescient gambler in 1908 and laid down cash on a big-league team rolling snake eyes for 105 straight seasons, today you'd be swimming in it, Scrooge McDuck–style. That is, if you were still alive. (The odds of that are approximately 250 million to 1.)

If there is a gate on this earth deserving of Dante's inscription *Lasciate ogne speranza, voi ch'intrate* (Abandon hope, all ye who enter here) it's Gate F at Wrigley Field. Yet, as they have every April since Wrigley opened in 1915, Cubs fans raise a collective middle finger to experience while they shuffle through it, their sense of hope firmly intact. "Come on, man," the chorus goes, "they're *due!*"

Over the preceding century-and-change, the Cubs have sold approximately 150 million tickets to these hope-addled—or if you prefer, hope-sustained—dreamers. Among them were my grandparents, Iowa farmers whose 1934 honeymoon trip east to Chicago included a game at Wrigley. The Cubs were a hot ticket then, just two years out from a National League pennant and in the thick of another race. Grandpa was disappointed by the Cubs' loss to the Cincinnati Reds, but he did return home with a souvenir ticket—as well as a souvenir sliver of wood he whittled from a phone pole outside the Biograph Theater, where John Dillinger had been shot just days before.

Grandpa and Grandma's next Cubs game was in 1945. This time they had two kids in tow. One of them was my eight-year-old dad. It was during that hopeful moment between VE Day and VJ Day. Wartime gasoline rationing had already ended, and Grandpa decided it was time for a celebratory trip to the Windy City. This time the Cubs won, beating the Pirates en route to another National League pennant. The Cubs would lose the '45 World Series to the Detroit Tigers, four games to three. It was their seventh straight World Series loss. Some blame Chicago restaurateur and Cubs fan Billy Sianis, who cursed the team after he and his pet goat were tossed from Wrigley during Game 4. Superstition or not, the Cubs haven't been to a World Series since.

Their National League pennant from that (cursed?) year today hangs near the salad bar at Wrigley's Stadium Club restaurant, a forlorn and barren senior citizen. I've had occasion to ponder the relic a few times since moving to Chicago. My first Cubs game was in 1969. I was an eight-year-old vacationing Iowa farm boy, just like my dad had been in 1945. Dad and Uncle Arlen treated me, my brother, and our cousins to a day

at Wrigley. It was a glorious victory by the first-place Cubs over
the Astros, the perfect introduction for a young boy to fandom.
And educational, too. The next month the Cubs underwent
the greatest collapse in Major League history and missed the
playoffs.

I eventually ended up living not far from Wrigley, and these
days I occasionally take my own boy to Cubs games—the sins of
the father being visited upon the son and all that. On *his* eighth
birthday—the date was October 14, 2003, which you may
recognize—the Cubs were about to close out a playoff series
against that ridiculous baseball club from Florida. In the eighth
inning, a well-meaning fan named Steve Bartman reached out
for a souvenir foul ball. There is some comfort in knowing
that my father, my son, and I learned the hard, eternal truth
about the Cubs at identical ages. Or at least that's what I tell
myself.

Despite all that, a lot of people in Chicago were stoked about
the Cubs' chances this year. Well, not this year, but maybe next.
Although the rebuilding could take longer. But playoff contenders by the midcentury, tops. You know how this hope stuff
goes.

A straight-thinking fan base would have thrown their support
behind a less depressing team fifty years ago. And by all conven-
tional lights, the Cubs would then have packed up and moved
to Orlando or Jacksonville or some other *arriviste* city in Florida
to get a better stadium deal and a fresh start. Yet deep inside,
no matter how grumpily and fatalistically he dismisses their
chances, even the most hard-bitten Wrigley bleacher bum truly,
truly believes that *this might finally be the year.*

The question, then, is why would anyone consider this sort
of historical, counterlogical, masochistic, Pollyanna belief a *vir-*

tue? From any objective standpoint, the Cubs fans' perennial, unshakeable hope really only benefits the team's front office. Hope is a virtue? Hell, it's a character flaw that leaves us prey to overpriced ball caps and eight-dollar cups of Old Style. If you're going to be purely rational about it, hope is for the gullible. The self-deluded. The suckers. Wise up, boy-o, *hope is for dopes.* It's nothing but a dressed-up, theologically approved version of the gambler's fallacy. Want to see hope at work? Walk through a casino floor in Las Vegas at eight o'clock in the morning. You'll see plenty of unshakeable hope in people's bloodshot eyes—every one of them genuinely believing they're just one lever pull, just one button push, just one dealer's face card or river turn from sweet deliverance. With virtue like that, who needs vice?

If you're going to *be* purely rational about it, the truly virtuous attitude would be to put a hand on the poor schlemiel's shoulder, buy him an all-you-can-eat breakfast, and explain how his faithful hope in the eventual charity of that roulette wheel is going to result in a trip to the pawnbroker and a long, smelly Greyhound ride back to Dubuque. In the words of the great twentieth-century theologian Kenny Rogers, "You've got to know when to hold 'em, know when to fold 'em, know when to walk away, and know when to run." Or, if we're going to switch metaphors back to the Cubbies, I should have sat my boy down and said, "Son, I know we live in Chicago, but geography doesn't have to be destiny. What are your feelings about pinstripes?"

If you're going to be purely *rational* about it, then our sanctification of hope as a cardinal virtue is less due to S. T. Aquinas than to P. T. Barnum. Which means that we'd do better training ourselves to follow enlightened self-interest rather than the pie-in-the-sky dreams of pie salesmen. Because let's face it, "Winners never quit and quitters never win" is a great motivational slogan—so long as you're playing with house odds. And it makes a difference whether that house is Caesar's Palace or Wrigley Field.

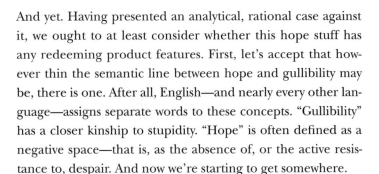

And yet. Having presented an analytical, rational case against it, we ought to at least consider whether this hope stuff has any redeeming product features. First, let's accept that however thin the semantic line between hope and gullibility may be, there is one. After all, English—and nearly every other language—assigns separate words to these concepts. "Gullibility" has a closer kinship to stupidity. "Hope" is often defined as a negative space—that is, as the absence of, or the active resistance to, despair. And now we're starting to get somewhere.

I wouldn't call despair a vice, exactly. All of us are, in some respect, susceptible to it. It's probably humankind's default position, actually. Just about everyone can look at the hollow-cheeked screamer in the Edvard Munch painting and think, *Been there, dude.* But if despair isn't a sin (except to Catholics; you know how they are), it's probably best seen as a weakness —as an instinct that, like fear, is perfectly human and logical— but that doesn't do us any favors in practical terms. If you get tossed in a pit with a rabid animal (or a Yankees fan) you have every reason to be afraid. But cowering in fear isn't going to help you survive. You have to master your fear, distract the animal, and then figure out a way to escape. (I suggest confusing them with a riddle. For instance, ask if they think Derek Jeter is omnipotent, and when they say yes—they always do—ask if Derek Jeter could make a hot dog so big that even Derek Jeter couldn't eat it. This should buy you a week or so.)

Hope involves the determination to transcend the crippling weakness of despair. Consider a lifeboat from a sunken ocean liner, adrift in the Pacific, with three survivors: a despairing pessimist, a hope-filled optimist, and yourself. The pessimist passes the time with constant reminders about the boat's dwindling supplies and by giving pet names to the sharks circling below. The optimist starts paddling, in the hope that maybe—just maybe—you'll catch a wave and be whisked away to an island paradise with movie starlets, hot Kansas farm girls, and a professor who can make shortwave radios from coconuts.

Now for the sake of argument, let's say the pessimist doomsayer was right all along and predicts with uncanny precision the exact day when all the food runs out. Now I can't speak for you, but when that moment comes I'm voting to eat *him.* In the end, Mr. Gloomy Cassandra's 100 percent accurate diagnoses may have bought him a brief moment of smug, triumphal I-told-you-so. But it gets followed by a few days as the featured dish on the lifeboat lunch menu. By contrast, no matter how wrong he turned out to be, Mr. Sunshine Pollyanna isn't going die regretting his optimism. The pessimist was correct, but even by his own cynical standard—*so what?* What did it benefit him? From the most self-interested perspective, even under the worst possible outcome, hope is ultimately the logical choice.

And then there's the other possibility: That the optimist turns out to be right. You make landfall and live out your days on a tropical paradise with Ginger on one arm and Mary Ann on the other. Either way, you're better off throwing in your lot with hope.

But of course those are just the practical reasons to give in to hope. The more philosophical argument concerns hope's ability to affect everyone aboard our shared cosmic lifeboat. Despair and hope are both contagious, perhaps equally so. If we are going to face a global attitudinal epidemic, better one of hopeful expectation than the alternative. Hope lays the foundation for the other virtues that advance humanity—courage, industry, exploration. And while hope may not be a plan, neither is despair. In fact, without hope, why bother with planning at all? Hope, or the lack thereof, can be a self-fulfilling prophecy, and a society that assumes an inevitably bleak future is going to get exactly what it expects. Sustaining hope benefits not only you but everyone around you—even those hopeless, eye-rolling cynics who remain immune to your good cheer. Whether they like it or not.

It isn't all puppy dogs and ice cream, mind you. Hope can, from time to time, leave people vulnerable to exploitation. Every good con artist, ad man, and political message consultant knows that "hope" has a boffo Q score. As always, caveat emptor. Here's a good rule of thumb for you kids: If something is branded "HOPE," then it's probably a swindle. Remember, there is no inherent contradiction between being hopeful and being skeptical; it's what separates hope from gullibility.

But just as a healthy bit of skepticism keeps hope from lapsing into gullibility, a healthy bit of hope keeps skepticism from lapsing into corrosive cynicism. Humankind is not neatly categorized with bright lines sectioning off the scheming grifters from the naive marks. You can't always tell Lucy from Charlie Brown. But instead of being on the constant lookout for the sharpies, it's probably best to recognize that the vast majority of this world is pretty much like you—good folks who just want things to turn out all right.

Which brings us back to the corner of Addison and Clark. I have to believe all the Cubs who've played there—from Kiki Kuyler and Phil Cavaretta, to Ernie Banks and Ron Santo, to Kerry Wood and Sammy Sosa—are as pained by the streak as I am. Even as they rake in all those millions in merchandise, TV, and beer revenue. I have to believe the Cubs front office wants to win the World Series every bit as much as I do. If only so the rest of the baseball world will leave us alone and start talking about the curse of the Cleveland Indians for a change. Hope may be a cardinal virtue, but it's also a Cubs virtue.

So maybe the Cubs won't win the World Series this year. Or next year. Maybe not in my dad's lifetime, maybe not in my lifetime. But eventually they will. I know this for a fact, because when the odds are above zero, everything is inevitable. And when that day comes, I'll raise the W flag from my celestial skybox and buy a round of Old Styles for Grandpa and Dad and Uncle Arlen. And we'll tell everybody who'll listen: We told you, man—they were *due*.

CHAPTER 7

Charity

You Can't Give This Stuff Away

Mollie Hemingway

THE INTERNET—stop me if you've heard this—is great for lots of things. Communication, wasting time, shopping, wasting time, research, wasting time, and finding pictures of cats getting into hilarious scrapes. (And also wasting time.) But one of the lesser-heralded features of the information superhighway—can you believe we used to call it that?—is the extent to which it has fostered and enabled charity. The ease of processing credit card payments online allows us to support charitable organizations anytime and anywhere. The advent of crowd-funding has allowed people to organize coordinated giving, leveraging the power of networks as a force multiplier. And then there's the speed of the Internet, which either triggers our charitable impulses or devalues charity to the state of impulse purchase, depending on your view. Either way, the upshot is that people now become passionately committed to causes they didn't know existed five minutes ago.

That's the futurist sales pitch. And maybe it's right—it's probably too soon to really understand the macro effects of the Internet on charitable giving. The Internet influence on actual *charity* is a little easier to get a handle on.

The Charities Aid Foundation publishes an annual global index of giving, rating 135 countries based on what percentage of the population donates money, volunteers time, and helps strangers. In the 2013 World Giving Index, the United States came out on top as the most generous nation. (A big comeback after being ranked fifth the year before. USA! USA!) That's great news, right? Well, not for everyone. In the comments section of one article about the World Giving Index results, the anonymous and eponymous weighed in. One mused about "cheap Christians." Another disparaged the Salvation Army for not being secular. Still another referred to "Euro misers" and called the Germans and British ugly names. The conversation, if it can be called that, quickly devolved into allegations that conservatives only give money if they can reasonably expect something in return and that liberals only give away other people's money. On the Internet, even a story about our financial generosity ends up as a demonstration of how uncharitable we are personally.

This isn't a new problem, mind you. "There is no dearth of charity in the world in giving, but there is comparatively little exercised in thinking and speaking." Or so wrote Sir Philip Sidney, way back in the sixteenth century, when they didn't even have PayPal. But the essence of the Internet is such that it takes these innate, if regrettable, impulses and encourages them in ways that Sir Philip couldn't possibly have imagined. The Web brings the world to your fingertips. In some ways this is great. The world is an interesting place. But there are lots of people in it, and if you've ever hung out at a bus station at three o'clock in the morning, you know that a fair number of them are loons. The Internet gives every one of those loons the ability to get right in front of your eyeballs. And the instantaneousness of it means that even the nonloons will sometimes (or often) not give the better angels of their nature time to assert themselves. Add crazy to instantaneous, then multiply that by the anonymity the Web affords, and the net result is there's nothing to stop anyone from saying whatever the heck pops into their mind, whether they just had three gin and tonics or are genuinely disturbed. And to make sure you see it.

If the Internet is a global village, then comments sections are the town square. And if you've never visited, believe me, it's a place where you don't want to roll down your window at night. Yet people are *fascinated* by them. Why is that? You wouldn't listen to someone named "PsychoBillyCadillac" in real life. But after reading a delightful article on the proper gardening techniques for peonies, there he is. PsychoBillyCadillac thinks peonies are *stupid*. "What kind of person would let *Paeonia* flower in their garden?" he wants to know. "Only fascist herbophobes plant peonies. True tolerance demands chrysanthemums."

And you get upset. Because you *really* like peonies. You've got a whole section of them right there, to the left of the koi pond. And here's PsychoBillyCadillac, jabbering at you while you sit in your living room with a cup of tea, insulting your flowers and calling you names. After his little rant, the other comments flow like a river, by turns snide, envious, enraged, vengeful, unrelenting, obsessive, and merciless. On the Internet, we call this lovely combination of attributes "snark."

As a mode of discourse, snark has eaten the Internet. The recipe for making it is simple enough: a dollop of sneering, a dash of bitter insults, scorn to taste, and then about five gallons of sarcasm to drown out any semblance of wit. But the most pernicious aspect of snark is that after consuming it day and night for years, it dulls the moral palate. It is, all on its own, a big part of why we've lost the ability to be gracious with one another.

And don't take my word for it—famous people see it the same way! The metabolism of the Internet is "a genuinely damaging force in our culture," muses the progressive screenwriter Aaron Sorkin:

> I don't think we're very nice to each other anymore . . . . There's just too much money to be made and too much fun to be had laughing at somebody else fail. And that's become okay. It used to be the kind of thing that you didn't do in public. . . . And now it's what covers . . . the homepage of the *Huffington Post.* "13 Epic #Fails." There's the need to put an exclamation point after everything, and there's the need to . . . create fantastic stories instead of just reporting on things. . . . So the adjectives and adverbs that you'll see in headlines are *always* about how somebody issued a *blistering* this against [someone or something]—just anything to get a clip.

Alec Baldwin feels pretty much the same way. After a series of run-ins with paparazzi who caught sight of his blistering temper, the actor published a grand essay saying good-bye to public life:

> In the New Media culture, anything good you do is tossed in a pit, and you are measured by who you are on your worst day. What's the Boy Scout code? Trustworthy. Loyal. Helpful. Friendly. Courteous. Kind. Obedient. Cheerful. Thrifty. Brave. Clean. Reverent. I might be all of those things, at certain moments. But people suspect that whatever good you do, you are faking. You're that guy. You're that guy that says this. There is a core of outlets that are pushing these stories out. Breitbart clutters the blogosphere with "Alec Baldwin, he's the Devil, he's Fidel Baldwin." . . . Even the U.S., which is so preposterously judg-

mental now. The heart, the arteries of the country are now clogged with hate. The fuel of American political life is hatred.

I know what you're thinking: *Boy, that is rich! Two of the angriest smarty-pants celebrities of the last twenty years think public life is too angry!* But the truth is that the vitriol they both saw boomerang back to them can be redirected to anyone, at any time.

On the Internet, every day is Festivus. Remember Festivus? It's the fictional holiday created by George Costanza's father on *Seinfeld*, the dinner celebration of which is capped by an "Airing of Grievances." George's father, Frank (played by the great Jerry Stiller), inaugurates the Airing of Grievances by shouting, "I got a lot of problems with you people! And now, you're gonna hear about it!" Well, we air grievances all day, every day, thanks to the Internet.

We can't hang it all on the Internet, though. Round-the-clock news on TV isn't helping either. Air time doesn't fill itself, you know, which is why we have every microscopic story—woman goes on rampage in McDonald's! Madonna offends millions with outrageous costume!—tarted up for gavel-to-gavel coverage. And if the "real" "news" wasn't bad enough, recent decades have seen the rise of "fake" news to boot.

The Daily Show is a satirical newscast, boasting millions of nightly viewers, and it is—as genuine newspapers often bleat masochistically—a primary source of news for many younger Americans. And it's not just self-hating newspapers puffing up the show. The Pew Foundation's "Project for Excellence in Journalism" concluded that "*The Daily Show* is clearly impacting American dialogue" and "getting people to think critically about the public square."

Nothing could be further from the truth, of course. To think critically means to judge carefully. *The Daily Show* makes critical thinking difficult, if not impossible, because of the industrial-strength snark that coats every aspect of the show.

Remember how Aaron Sorkin pointed out that the adjectives and adverbs you'll see in headlines are always about how somebody issued a "blistering" attack? Here's a sampling of recent headlines about *The Daily Show*: "Jon Stewart Slams . . . ," "Jon Stewart Blasts . . . ," "Jon Stewart Rips . . . ," "Jon Stewart Goes Off . . . ," "Jon Stewart Is Shocked . . . ," "Jon Stewart Rips . . ." (again), "Jon Stewart Can't Deal with Idiots . . . ," "Jon Stewart Rips . . ." (yet again), "Jon Stewart Hits . . . ," "Jon Stewart Mocks . . . ," "Jon Stewart Rips . . ." (still again), and "Jon Stewart Calls Out. . . ." You get the picture.

All of those headlines were taken from a single website, the *Huffington Post* (give Sorkin another gold star) over a three-month period. There is no intellectual charity on *The Daily Show*. It is simply an exercise in pandering to an audience that needs to feel superior and to political elites whose positions the show's staff support. All arguments from political enemies are assumed to be in bad faith, and ad hominem is standard operating procedure.

Satire can be a wonderfully persuasive tool. However, satire and irony lose all impact when they're part of our constant cultural diet and present in nearly all political discourse. Meaningful communication is rendered impossible.

Whether it's the real media, social media, or fake news shows, we have a charity problem in our culture.

The comedian Louis C. K. has a riff about why he won't buy a phone with Internet capability for his daughters. His rationale? He wants them to learn empathy. "You know, kids are mean . . .

They look at a kid and they go, 'You're fat,' and then they see the kid's face scrunch up and they go, 'Oh, that doesn't feel good to make a person do that,'" C. K. says. "But when they write, 'You're fat' [on the Internet, from their smartphone], then they just go, 'Mmm, that was fun, I like that.'"

Whether he knows it or not, C. K. is echoing Aquinas, among others, in understanding that proximity plays a role in charity. It used to be a cliché that charity begins at home. As Aquinas (quoting Augustine) put it, "Since one cannot do good to all, we ought to consider those chiefly who, by reason of place, time, or any other circumstance, by a kind of chance are more closely united to us."

Charity was always understood as a relationship between real people. It's impossible to love all of humanity. It's hard enough to love those closest to us—our insufferable siblings, our annoying colleagues, the next-door neighbors who sometimes step on our peonies. The reason the Internet has so demolished the idea of charity is simple: When everyone's your neighbor, then nobody's your neighbor.

But wait—there's more! Saint Peter pushed charity not just for the receiver but for the sake of the giver: "Above all things have fervent charity among yourselves: for charity shall cover the multitude of sins."

What he's driving at is that charity assumes errors and misdeeds not just on the part of our neighbors but also on ourselves. As Aleksandr Solzhenitsyn put it in *The Gulag Archipelago,* "If only there were evil people somewhere insidiously committing evil deeds, and it were necessary only to separate them from the rest of us and destroy them. But the line dividing good and evil cuts through the heart of every human being. And who is willing to destroy a piece of his own heart?"

In the old days, back before dial-up modems, we would be charitable to our neighbor in the same way we hoped he'd be charitable toward us when we weren't our best selves. But the other thing the Internet has done away with is the very idea of there being a "best" self. There's just you. And you're free to be you any way you want. This narrow view of sin, it turns out, leads to an extremely narrow view of charity.

We even feel it in the home. It is darkly humorous that so many Christian couples choose to have 1 Corinthians 13:4 read at their wedding—you know, the "love is patient, love is kind" litany. But the better translation for the word "love" in that passage is, as P. J. O'Rourke noted a few pages back, "charity." So, in the beautiful prose of the King James Bible, Saint Paul writes, "Charity suffereth long, and is kind; charity envieth not; charity vaunteth not itself, is not puffed up; Doth not behave itself unseemly, seeketh not her own, is not easily provoked, thinketh no evil; Rejoiceth not in iniquity, but rejoiceth in the truth; Beareth all things, believeth all things, hopeth all things, endureth all things." And so on and so forth.

Then as if directly rebuking *The Daily Show*—not to mention each and every one of us—Saint Paul continues, "When I was a child, I spake as a child, I understood as a child, I thought as a child: but when I became a man, I put away childish things. For now we see through a glass, darkly; but then face to face: now I know in part; but then shall I know even as also I am known. And now abideth faith, hope, charity, these three; but the greatest of these is charity."

It's the perfect verse for marrying couples, but not because it's about romantic love. Charity is about what happens when romantic love fails. It's about what happens when people don't agree with your beliefs. When people make jokes that fail. When celebrities have a bad day.

How much better our intellectual, public, and even home life would be if charity were the watchword. If we assumed the best of people's motives instead of the worst. If we grappled with their best arguments rather than their worst. If we assumed that those who disagree with us are neither evil (as liberals often see conservatives) or stupid (as conservatives often see liberals).

Above all, if we'd only acknowledge that all of us are mistaken from time to time, then we'd be more willing to forgive others in the hopes they will extend the same measure of charity to us.

CHAPTER 8

Faith

The Eleventh Commandment

Larry Miller

THE DESIGNATED HITTER is a great rule. Or a stupid rule. Let's fight about it.

Turn here, it's shorter. Sez you, it's longer. So's your old man. That woman is beautiful. No, she's not. Put 'em up, baldy. God will help us. There is no God. Shut up.

Taxes are—oh, you get the point. People love to argue.

The smartest, toughest, kindest, hardest-working, most patriotic, and generous people in America today—that's you and me, by the way—can only agree on one thing: Anything worth fighting for . . . is worth fighting for.

Speaking of God, this chip on the shoulder goes back to the Garden of Eden, where the very beginning was almost the very end. You're in a beautiful place, the ruler of all you see, plenty to eat, the weather's perfect, you like her, she likes you, nothing for the two of you to do all day but (oh, come on, you know). Yes, everything is as high as an elephant's eye, but . . . uh-oh! The Commander in Chief gives the first man and the first woman the first order, and they blissfully disobey him.

DON'T EAT FROM THE TREE OF KNOWLEDGE. YOU TWO ARE FORBIDDEN TO EAT FROM THE TREE OF KNOWLEDGE. WOULD YOU PLEASE STOP STARING AT HER FOR TEN SECONDS AND LISTEN TO ME? NEVER, EVER, *EVER, EVER* EAT FROM THE TREE OF KNOWLEDGE.

You know what happened then, and it's pathetic, really. Come on, the Creator of heaven and earth hands you everything on a silver platter, asks that you obey one simple rule, and what's the first thing you do after naming the animals? Eat from the Tree of Knowledge. So your opinion counts more than His? No need to chat about it with the Big Fella? There's just no God or something?

Oops. Whoa. Hold the wire. Yikes.

Is it even possible that . . . there is no God? This should've been solved a long time ago, but it's apparently still sitting on the coffee table like a brand-new book. Let's calm down and ask it plain as day. Is there a God, or isn't there?

Ah, but there's more!

Let's not just ask it. Let's solve it. You and me. Right now.

No need to panic, it's a big issue with two sides. So let's examine both, one at a time, and I'll bet you we easily see who's right. Here we go. Ready?

The first proposition is: There is no God. Okay, if there is no God, then He/She/It/Them doesn't exist and never has. Nothing was created or planned or conceived or guided, and everything just grew and changed on its own, including you.

All the big rules in life were thought up by chubby men with beards, and the ceiling in the Sistine Chapel may have lots of paint on it, but it started and ended in Michelangelo's noggin and none of it's true. (The good news is that's the last time I'll have to look up Sistine and Michelangelo to see how they're spelled.) Don't worry about "the other side of life," because you're already in it. There is no other side. And if you're waiting for Judgment Day, start today and judge yourself.

Speaking of which, there is no Judgment Day, or Judgment Night, or any judgment at all. You don't have to stand in line at a Pearly Gate waiting to get in, and no cheerful assistant with a full head of shiny hair and a clipboard will stroll with you over to God's office for the big "Where Do You Spend Eternity" meeting, yakking about this and that on the way, and pointing out new trees and fresh paint on the fairy-tale stores, while you stand there open-jawed and thunderstruck at how much Main Street looks like Disney World.

(Like, a LOT. I mean, they even have a cute red train on adorable tracks that puffs around the place and you can't help wondering if the one up here still has that pirate chasing the waitress around the drinking table. Because maybe old Walt's avuncular smile meant a lot more than we thought.)

How's it feel so far? A little unsettling? You ain't seen nothin' yet.

No God, no heaven, no nothing. No need to worry about eternity, because there is none. No chance to be the trillionth soul to tell Shakespeare how great he was, no opportunity to tell Helen of Troy how super-duper pretty she is, like, so-*so*-**so** gorgeous (and just your type, really) and would she like to have dinner with you tonight so you can tell her fortune? No reason to hunt down all the modern twentieth-century composers and tell them how you never liked their arhythmic, atonal music, but do they know where Puccini and Verdi and Bach hang out? You'll never meet Beethoven or Saint Agnes or Babe Ruth or Charlemagne or Jerry Garcia or Hedy Lamarr. You'll never meet all the girls you struck out with in high school just to say hi to them and apologize and catch up and—who knows?—maybe take one more shot.

Bottom line: You'll never meet . . . well, anyone.

No afterlife, no lessons of life, no heroes of life, no day-dreaming in your coffin, no thinking, no planning, no praying, no breathing, no life, no God. NO GOD.

Your parents aren't waiting for you with arms held out and perfect love, and your grandparents and uncles and aunts and friends aren't there with smiles so pure it makes you cry. Every cloud really does have a silver lining, though, so here's some good news. Since there's no Big Meeting with the King of Kings, He will not be striding into it glaring at you while carrying a file that's *way* thicker than you thought it would be. Plus, you won't have to watch Him get madder and madder as you make excuses that even you don't believe, while He drums His fingers on a spot on His desk that definitely looks like it's seen a lot of loud finger-drumming before. (It has.)

More good news! You won't have to worry about your wife and kids back on Earth, because no such bonds exist. There is no forever; they're on their own. Let 'em wipe the mud off their own boots.

You won't have to worry about the secrets of life, because they don't exist. You won't have to worry about final battles or Armageddon or good and evil or who's right and who's wrong, or whether your parents ever knew you snuck that girl into your bedroom in tenth grade, or anything.

Oh, sure, there'll be a little sadness that this is the end, and it came so fast, and there's nothing more, but if the best people in history hit the same emptiness, you can, too. If the point in life is that there is no point in life—and no point in yours—you can take it. Right? RIGHT?

And there are no fights about religion, because there is no religion.

I know this is all a little blunt, but here's the good side to having no God. You're not only responsible for yourself—you're *completely* responsible. Step up and serve. There's no one watching your back and saving your hide. If you loved your parents, fine; if you hated them, fine. It doesn't matter. Deal with life yourself. Save starving people or bomb them. No one's watching and no one cares. Don't let anyone tell you anything. You tell them. Honor your wife and stay faithful, but if you're on the road and you meet a hot divorcée, invite her up to your room and empty the minibar. Why not? Work hard, but steal all you can. Who cares? Smoke wherever you want.

The bad guys don't get punished, and the good guys don't get anything.

No light, no love, no lessons, no ladders, no robes, no wings, no hugs, no meaning. No truth. No God.

But that's only one side. Here's the other: First, take five, throw some water on your face, check to see if the kids are doing their homework or playing a game (of course they're playing a game, dummy), grab a beer, go back downstairs, and take another breath. Here we go. The second proposition: There is a God.

(Oh, and this time, smile.)

There is a God, there is a light, and your parents really are waiting for you with arms held out and perfect love. It's the single most thrilling sight in creation. Right next to them are your grandparents and all the relatives and friends you always cared about, and yes, their smiles are as moving as anything has ever been, and your hugs with them take a long, long time. Behind them are all the ancestors you've never met going back in history to the very beginning, and their smiles and hugs are great, too, because they wanted so much to meet you. They all look, well, beautiful, just the right ages, just the right clothes, and you laugh and laugh and laugh together.

Everything you've just seen and done is so moving it's almost impossible to imagine that so many on Earth don't believe it.

You return to your parents' arms, and they whisper, "Of course we knew about that girl in your bedroom. What are we, stupid? By the way, the dogs are here, too! Pierre and Senator and Desdi and Dawg and Norman, all of them." No one's rushing you through this, because everyone knows that for the first time in your life you have all the time in the world to love and be loved.

How much time? Eternity. But this is just the first step.

Your parents walk you over to a pool of water and point, and now you have a perfect vision of your family back on Earth. They are home after your funeral and are tired and sad, but they're happy, too, because they're each holding something of yours, a book, a football, sneakers, and they're laughing, because the boys are drinking Cokes, and you always said that was no good for them, and they always said it was, and you always said, "No!" Then you shrug and have a Coke, too, and give them all fresh ones, and say, "Boy, nothing beats a Coke," and one of the boys gets a big bag of potato chips from the pantry to go with it, and that's the way it always, always happened. And they're doing it now in memory and smiling, and you begin to weep.

No bonds? Good Lord, they're the strongest bonds in the universe. The bonds with your parents and wife and children are as deep as the ocean and last forever, and your parents hold you close now as they did when you were a baby, and it finally hits you that's exactly what you are now. You're a baby again.

They all walk you to meet God in His office for the Big Meeting, and it turns out Main Street really is beautiful and does look like Disney World.

Of course there's a God, and of course there's a Big Meeting. It's your Judgment Day, and God may have a sour look on His face (He always does), and that's right, your file may be far thicker than you thought it would be. (Everyone's is.)

That's okay, though, because here's a surprise that's very good and very big. Yes, the Lord is known for His quick temper, but it's far more important when you realize He gives good people, all good people, and you, too, all the time they need to ask forgiveness. That's what really counts.

You see, bad people get punished deeply. And with them the Big Meeting doesn't take long at all, but oh, how they wish it did. As soon as He walks in, they get it and understand, and crumble and scream and instantly know the depth of the evil they committed, and feel it all for the first time. They're crushed with sadness and waste and judgment and fear, and the reason that meeting is so short and nothing is said is that there's nothing to say. The bad ones have a very long time to think about that.

Bad people don't even need to hear their verdicts; they already know them. They knew it in this life, too, but they were too stubborn to pay them any mind. Then, finally, at the end of the very short meeting, the bad people stand and leave and are taken to an elevator by the same assistant (who's no longer smiling), and the streets aren't beautiful anymore but dark and cold and empty, and as soon as the bad people enter the elevator they notice they're alone, and their sadness multiplies greatly, because they know they'll be alone forever, and they realize what every other monster in history knows: The old, old elevator has no buttons, and it only goes one way—down—at one speed—fast—and the worst truth of all, no matter how horrible the place is that they're going, is that the elevator will never, ever take them back up.

Folks, friends, it's time to learn that you definitely want a long meeting with God, because if you have one, you've already made it. You're in! Even the greatest, finest people in history had long meetings with God.

Right after your parents hug you (and that's a pretty good hug, by the way) they tell you heaven is far bigger than you thought, and all the good souls have more work to do, and it's very important work. It's God's work, and both He and they and you have never been happier.

There is another side of life. Of course there is; nothing would make sense without it. There is a Judgment Day, there is a heaven up high. There's lots of religion, and you finally learn that doesn't mean sitting stiffly in starched clothes—it means reaching out yourself, because prayers are love songs. It turns out you can meet Beethoven and Saint Agnes and all your heroes. You can meet them for eternity. And sure, Helen of Troy may not be interested in you, but who knows?

Your meeting with God doesn't start with Him mad, either. You look up when He comes in and realize your parents aren't the only ones with their arms held out in perfect love. God does, too, and it's all you can do to stand up shaking and move to Him, and God's hug is so good you don't even mind when His first question is, "So what was the deal with that girl in your bedroom in tenth grade? You kissed for a while, like two clumsy kids, but nothing else happened, and why would it? How was that climb back out the window afterward? You broke that screen, didn't you? Of course your parents knew about it. You're lucky hers didn't."

Every soul is valuable. Shakespeare is just as pleased with you as you are with him, and, holy moly, wonder of wonders, can you believe it? Helen of Troy thinks you're a cutie pie and has a few things she'd like to read to you, too.

Every hug and conversation and song last forever, you can do them all at the same time, they never conflict, everyone walks together.

It turns out a prayer is just speaking right to God, and He hears everything, and you're perfect for that, too. Your mom and dad are so loved by God they get big promotions. They can't tell you where they go, but you know it's good, and you're just happy they're there. (Maybe someday you'll go somewhere wonderful, too.)

There are many secrets in heaven, but each one is a great joy when you understand. And you understand.

Watching a sunset on Earth is beautiful, but not even close to watching angels slowly float by. Kissing a beautiful woman on Earth isn't a trillionth as good as seeing a child in heaven laughing with a dog. A bite of fresh pizza in heaven seems to be the best taste anyone's ever had. And it is. No one has trouble sleeping in heaven, and no one has trouble waking up . . . *and the dreams!* Heaven is a movie, a constant movie, the best movie ever, and it's still being made, and you're in it, and it's great every time you see it. There are no surprise endings because the movie never stops.

Maybe the best of all is that hug from God, though, so complete, so pure, so right, and there's no way to learn anything about it except to do it. Even the greatest writers in heaven, when asked to describe God's hug, simply smile and say, "Go to heaven and get His hug."

I told a friend once he should definitely believe in God with no hesitation. I said, "Look at it this way. If there's no God and no judgment and no Heaven and nothing, you haven't lost anything, you just lived a better life. You're as dead as everyone, no harm, no foul. But if there is? If there's a God and Judgment and the whole nine yards, and you're walking to the Big Meeting with the Big Fella and you see how big your file is? Well, whoa, come on, there you are, the fair-haired boy with a lot of gold stars on his record and way ahead in points, and in that Big Meeting the first thing you say can be, 'Just want you to know, I was with you the whole way.'"

Now, God's still going to know you're yanking Him a bit, but any way it shakes out, it's way better to believe.

So that's it. We're finished. Those are the two possibilities: There is a God, or there isn't. You may be saying, "No! Wait! More, more! We haven't found the answer!"

Oh, but we have. It's called faith. Of course there's a God. I think there is. I know there is. You do, too. Everything makes sense that way, and the difficult questions on Earth are obvious in heaven. What do you want? Emptiness or joy; boredom or wonder; nothing or everything? We wouldn't have love down here if we didn't get it up there.

The next time someone says, "There is no God, and nothing can change my mind." Just smile and say, "Go to heaven and get His hug."

Maybe that's what it said in the Book of Knowledge. No pictures, no promises, no threats. Just one white page, and it says, "The Eleventh Commandment: Go to heaven and get His hug."

Part II

The Everyday Virtues

The ones your grandmother told you about
but you ignored.
Because they're no fun.
Trust us.

CHAPTER 9

Chastity

The Final Taboo

Matt Labash

THOUGH ADMITTEDLY not a professional historian, I do watch a lot of the History Channel—now that it mostly programs reality shows, instead of all that dreary business about the past. With my semiprofessional credentials thus authenticated, I feel it incumbent upon me to mark the historical moment when our nation became conclusively, irrefragably slutty. Or at least the moment in which it occurred to me.

It wasn't in the Roaring Twenties, when flappers, tight on bathtub gin, started hiking up their newly shortened skirts in the backseats of Model Ts. Nor was it in the swinging key parties of the Quaaluded and Qiana-draped seventies. To me, the realization of our overwhelming sluttitude dawned in the year 2000 (I'm not the quickest study), during the Republican National Convention.

I was ostensibly there to cover it, meaning I was mostly on the lookout for oddities and open-bar parties, while my more sober journalistic colleagues suffered through speeches from the electrifying likes of George Pataki and Tom Ridge. But my nose for news took me to a dirty bookstore in Philadelphia, a place in which I ordinarily wouldn't be caught dead, on account of all the clammy-palmed perverts you meet there. (Not in the dirty bookstore—in Philadelphia, I mean.)

The Scorpio Adult Bookstore wasn't just a book/video store,

but a full-service sex shop, complete with strippers plying their trade in peep booths—the kind of establishment where you wished you'd worn cleated hiking boots instead of loafers. I arrived along with a media pal named Lexxx Rubba. (That's not his real name, but to protect the "innocent," all friends appearing in this chapter have been given aliases originating from a porn-star name generator.) We had come to see a convention-themed political question-and-answer session with the legendary porn actress Nina Hartley. Think of her as the Judi Dench of the one-handed film world, with star turns in the likes of *Minivan Moms 12: Cougar Edition* and *Woodworking 101: Nina's Guide to Better Fellatio.*

Hartley, who grew up a brainy, red-diaper baby, is a "sex-positive" feminist who, when not rutting for money in drafty warehouses in the San Fernando Valley, likes to crank out essays for turgid anthologies with titles such as "Frustrations of a Feminist Porn Star." Standing between racks of culturally diverse porn videos, from *White Trash Whore 3* to *Black Knockers Volume 60,* Hartley had some political thoughts she wanted to share with the small crowd—all men—who had flocked around her. She prattled on for a spell, fretting that George W. Bush was in the pocket of the religious right. She enthused over Bill Clinton, "a highly sexed man, I like that in my leaders." Though she scrupulously added that, regarding his Monica problem, "oral sex *is* sex," thus authoritatively settling the most pressing intellectual debate of the 1990s.

It probably warrants mentioning that while Hartley was holding forth, she stood before us buck naked, except for a pair of stiletto heels and tastefully understated nail polish. Lexxx and I labored not to elbow each other. But as she droned on about the terrifying prospects of Bush's Supreme Court appointments, she began scratching her crotch. Not subtle scratching, either. She scratched like a third-base coach with a chigger infestation.

Maybe it's my biological wiring. Maybe it's that I was raised Southern Baptist, where we like to keep our guilty pleasures a little guiltier. (Baptists believing that there's no other kind of pleasure.) But I generally prefer women who are a tad less in-your-face. I've never been too keen on strippers or porn stars, since something about a stranger working that hard to turn my crank makes me unbearably sad. Lexxx, on the other hand, is a lusty satyr, especially when his blood-alcohol concentration is north of .30, which it happened to be during the entirety of convention week. And Lexxx, it should be said, generally likes his women the way he likes his liquor—promiscuously offered. But as Hartley kept itching, even Lexxx was prompted to lean over and whisper, "Good Lord, let's get out of here."

What bothered me, however, wasn't the scratching. Nor Hartley herself. After all, when you think about it, why should she be scandalized by her own public nudity while discussing the lack of dynamism in future Secretary of Labor Elaine Chao? Hartley is, after all, a trained, professional pornographer. For her, getting worked up over nudity would be like a plumber getting agitated over a basin wrench. What struck me was that nobody else batted an eye at the spectacle of a birthday-suited porn star solemnly holding forth on Al Gore's electoral chances. The assembled gents didn't even seem particularly invested in her as an object of desire. Sure, a few took pictures with her, sliding their hands to places most HR departments don't permit. (She willingly, if joylessly, let them.) But otherwise they might have been getting ready to phone into C-SPAN. They were blasé and businesslike, as if they see this sort of thing everyday. And with the Internet having turned America into a 24/7 porn emporium, they pretty much do.

The jaded, ho-humness of it all made me realize how far we'd fallen. Here they were, staring one of our debased culture's most treasured icons of sexual athleticism right in the face (among other parts). And yet, anything approaching actual sexiness had been subtracted from the equation. "Sex" in this context, was coarse and blunt and transactional—a once-juicy plum now dehydrated into a prune.

As another friend, Daddy Jammer (porn-star generator name), puts it,

> The underreported problem with a society that places no limits on sex is that after a while, it dulls desire. For the same reason there aren't many hard-ons in a nudist colony, a sex-soaked society gets boring after a while. I see it even with my own son. He's only sixteen, but he seems way less anxious about sex than I did at twenty-one, probably because in his world, they're giving away blowjobs, and he knows it. And there's always porn if they aren't. It worries me. It's like he's too calm—the calm before the boredom. Or as my father once put it, "The problem with pornography is that it's numbing. After a while, you can't get it up unless you're wearing a chicken costume."

Which brings us to the virtue at hand, chastity. If you go by the received wisdom, chastity is the thick-ankled stepsister of virtues. The wallflower with the wart on her nose, the last one to get asked to the dance. With an identical beginning and ending, along with the same number of syllables, chastity has the phonetic ring of the sexier virtue, charity. Except when you practice charity, you get pats on the back and deductions on your taxes. Being chaste just gets you odd looks and suspected of being a weirdo.

If we even say "chastity" anymore (which we mostly don't), it's purely by accident. Like when discussing the gender reassignment surgery of Cher's beefy former daughter, Chastity Bono (now her beefy son, Chaz). It has a fusty archaic-ness. Saying it out loud sounds like you're putting on airs, or like you're trying to employ words from the same family as "peradventure" or "soothfast," mothballed relics of a bygone time.

Chastity, of course, can be defined numerous ways. In the classic Christian understanding, it tends to mean sexual purity outside of marriage—that is, no premarital intercourse. (Though as Professor Hartley stipulates, the definition of "sex" can be a bit more elastic.) If you're a certain stripe of cleric, say, a Catholic priest, it can mean embracing a far scarier notion—lifetime celibacy, leaving even believers like me to pray that if I'm ever called to ministry, it's as a Protestant. And if you're married, it means fidelity, or put another way, making sweet monkey love to your heart's content, so long as that monkey love stays within the confines of your marriage. Though even here, there is some debate about what exactly being "chaste" entails. Especially since Christ, whose work I'm a tremendous fan of otherwise, left the gate wide open in His otherwise flawless Sermon on the Mount, when He said, "That whosoever looketh on a woman to lust after her hath committed adultery with her already in his heart."

Which, technically speaking, makes me a serial adulterer every time my wife's Victoria's Secret catalog arrives in the mail. I take comfort in the fact that Christ also said, "Let he who hath not [lusted after Alessandra Ambrosio] cast the first stone." A loose translation, admittedly, but it is in the Bible. Go ahead and Google it.

Because of its inherent difficulty, chastity, unlike most other virtues, has taken a kick in the shorts even from plenty of literary and theological giants. Aldous Huxley called it "the most unnatural of all sexual perversions." C. S. Lewis admitted it was "the most unpopular of the Christian virtues." Saint Augustine confessed in his *Confessions* that in his youthful days, he prayed, "Grant me chastity and continence, but not yet." Not to be outdone, Madonna (the slutty singer from Detroit, not Jesus's mom) said, "It is difficult to believe in a religion that places such a high premium on chastity and virginity."

These days, if you do dare place a premium on chastity—and not even the church or dictionary definitions, but just as a yellow light of caution to say, "Slow down, don't be so slutty"—you're liable to get called "puritanical." Or worse. Though there really isn't any worse obloquy today, since in our sex-addled society, Puritanism is synonymous with being a joyless, sexless prude. (On campuses, for instance, abstinence advocates are often treated like lepers or College Republicans.) Never mind that this isn't quite historically fair to the Puritans. It's not like they were celibate Shakers, electing to nonbreed themselves straight out of existence. The average Puritan household used to be good for around seven children apiece—meaning that ol' Artemus and Temperance were clearly up to more than just listening to Cotton Mather sermons, conducting witch trials, and singing rounds of "Grace! 'Tis a Charming Sound."

Not that we need to ride too high in the moralist's saddle. C. S. Lewis—nobody's idea of a libertine—argued, "If anyone thinks Christians regard unchastity as the supreme vice, he is quite wrong. The sins of the flesh are bad, but they are the least bad of all sins." Much worse, he wrote, were spiritual "pleasures"—backbiting, hatred, the joy of putting others in the wrong. He divided the two classes into sins of the flesh ("the Animal self") vs. sins of the spirit ("the Diabolical self"), about which he added, "The Diabolical self is the worse of the two. That is why a cold self-righteous prig who goes regularly to church may be far nearer to hell than a prostitute. But, of course, it is better to be neither."

Still, even by the middle of his century, Lewis saw how the backlash against "Puritanism" was overcorrecting the train right off the rails: "They tell you sex is a mess because it was hushed up. But for the last twenty years it has not been hushed up. It has been chattered about all day long. Yet it is still in a mess." Sexual desire in itself is the most natural of natural things, and in its proper place, even has a biblical seal of amorous approval, as anyone who has read the (Fifty Shades of) Song of Solomon knows: "Your stature is like that of the palm, and your breasts like clusters of fruit. I said, 'I will climb the palm tree; I will take hold of its fruit.'"

Yet, as Lewis understood, "Every sane and civilized man must have some set of principles by which he chooses to reject some of his desires and to permit others. . . . Surrender to all our desires obviously leads to impotence, jealousies, lies, conceal-ment, and everything that is the reverse of health, good humor, and frankness. For any happiness in this world, quite a lot of restraining is going to be necessary."

Sex, to Lewis's thinking, was a lot like food: "There is nothing to be ashamed of in enjoying your food: there would be every-thing to be ashamed of if half the world made food the main interest of their lives and spent their time looking at pictures of food and dribbling and smacking their lips." He published these words in the 1940s, perhaps not even anticipating the ter-minus of the sex/food analogy. Now, we not only ogle pictures all day—Internet porn consumption is so commonplace that, according to *Christianity Today*, even 40 percent of Christian ministers are said to struggle with it—but we have become so sluttified that we don't just smack our lips and dribble down our bibs. We ask for thirds and fourths, lick the plate clean, and then eat the flatware.

I should stipulate straightaway that calling America "slutty" is by no means implicative of a specific gender. It's not just women. Calling a man a slut is, as all men know, very near a tautology. But I do so purely to inoculate myself against the rabid bites of sharp-fanged postfeminists at places like the website Jezebel, which dominate "the debate," such as it is. They've made "slut-shaming" a fighting word, but the trick is, it's not an insult leveled at sluttiness, but rather toward the shamers. (There being nothing more shameful than having shame.) Classic feminists used to cry for sexual liberation while decrying the oppressive objectification of a patriarchal hegemony (their words, not mine; I prefer English), whereas the new breed—the second- and third-wavers—are quite happy to "objectify" themselves under the guise of "empowerment."

So with no remaining sense of chastity or inhibition, how slutty have we become as a culture? Let's take a quick tour.

Celebrity sex tapes are now so pervasive (Paris Hilton, Hulk Hogan, John Edwards—the list is long and undistinguished) that it's a buyer's market. *TMZ* recently reported that there were no takers on Indianapolis Colts running back Trent Richardson's orgy tape featuring the NFL player and three women. Perhaps the Kardashians had already flooded the zone. Remember, their whole seedy, tabloid cover–bait empire launched when the otherwise talent-free Kim Kardashian got "caught" on tape.

Even our former Disney stars behave like porn stars these days (see Miley Cyrus, she of the perpetually probing tongue, who has yet to meet a surface, inanimate or otherwise, that she won't lasciviously twerk). On any given day, either Cyrus,

Vanessa Hudgens, or any number of other former role models for young tweens are busy posting naked or nearly naked selfies online. A recent survey found one-third of all young adults have sexted or posted nude or seminude pictures of themselves. Even the guys want in on the action. Dylan Sprouse, former star of Disney's *The Suite Life of Zach & Cody*, recently posted a nude selfie of him, in a mirror, cupping his manhood. He sounded just sick about it afterward, too, when tweeting, "Whoops, guess I'm not 14 and fat anymore." He also noted that it helped him gain two hundred thousand more Twitter followers, Twitter-porn perhaps being the only porn more addictive than porn-porn.

Such ho-baggery on the part of young female celebrities even prompted a rare fellow-celebrity outcry from actress Rashida Jones, who tweeted #stopactinglikewhores, and who later penned a screed for *Glamour* magazine decrying the "pornification of everything." Jones called 2013 the "Year of the Very Visible Vagina," and suggested that cynically exploitative entertainment execs should seek ways to make women feel good about other qualities they possess, such as "I don't know . . . our empathy, or childbearing skills, or ability to forgive one another for mean tweets." For her troubles, Jones was practically drawn and quartered in the public square (mostly by other women) because, apparently, she had no shame at being a slut-shamer.

But celebrities, who are exhibitionists by trade, aren't the only ones acting like porners. So are the rest of us. From tramp stamps to penis tattoos (yes, people get them), everyone gets inked like porn stars these days. (In the world of pornography, 45.5 percent of performers have tats; in the real world the figure is 36 percent, with women outnumbering men in some surveys.) We dress ourselves like porners. One designer recently came up with the "Backtacular," a "gluteal cleft shield" to cover the plumber's cleavage that rises like the moon over the low-cut pants favored by Cool Moms who can't understand why their daughters dress so slutty (as they take off to the gym for stripper-pole classes in see-through Lululemons).

We dress our children like porners, in "babykinis" (string-bikinis for babies), or push-up bikini tops for girls too young to have breasts (courtesy of Abercrombie & Fitch), or a whole slew of "future porn star"–themed onesies and T-shirts—widely available on the Internet—for the slutty toddlers looking to get a leg up on the slutty teens and the slutty adults we're teaching them to become.

In fact, we've become so accustomed to dressing like porners that now we even undress like them. Taking to its natural extreme last decade's trend of wearing the sluttiest Halloween costume possible, one coed at Arizona State University recently arrived at a Halloween frat party dressed in nothing except a pair of heels. Pictures of the festivities spread across the Internet. As a writer named "Bacon" (not his Christian name, we assume) noticed from the website Total Frat Move, "There weren't even a pair of ears to make her a Slutty Leopard or Slutty Rabbit. I guess she was just a Slutty Slut. Not sure, don't care, because NAKED." With feminist logic like that—feminism and frat-boyism are often indistinguishable these days—Bacon could have been angling for an internship at Jezebel.

How slutty are we? Well, in the old days, if you wanted a quick hit and didn't have the skills to wow the ladies at the Greene Turtle happy hour, you could pay for a prostitute. But now, people are eagerly willing to prostitute themselves with "hook-up apps" such as Tinder and Pure, which help you get straight to the rutting with willing participants in your geographic vicinity, without any of the bother of having a conversation or learning their name. So rampant is the hook-up culture on most college campuses that Boston College offered a course on how to plan a date, dating being nearly as forgotten as chastity.

Middle-aged journalists, of course, love to bemoan the promiscuity of the college hook-up culture, since part of the fun of getting old is complaining how the youth of today are destroying civilization. But the hook-up culture doesn't end when you graduate. A spokesperson for AshleyMadison.com, the world's largest married hook-up service, where married folks go to cheat on their spouses (company slogan: "Life is short, have an affair"), announced they had 27,511 new sign-ups on New Year's Day 2014—a 344 percent spike over normal days. This is like the entire population of Helena, Montana, simultaneously deciding on the same day that cheating on their spouse would be their New Year's resolution.

You can see why marriage is becoming as endangered as dating. In fact, nearly four in ten respondents in a recent Pew Survey said they thought marriage was becoming "obsolete." (There are presently thirty-one marriages for every one thousand unmarried women in the United States, down from ninety in the 1950s.) Not that this is stopping anyone from making babies. The out-of-wedlock birthrate in America now hovers just above 40 percent (it's close to 50 percent for first births), which is bad news for a large swath of the newborns who hope their parent(s) are able to afford babykinis and future-porn-star onesies.

How slutty have we become? So slutty that people now try using chastity to sell sex. Hit the bookstore racks these days and you don't see chastity talked about in the context of abstinence-promotion programs or purity rings, as was once all the rage. (Even Miley Cyrus wore one in her Disney days; it didn't take.) Instead, you're more likely to see Georgia Ivey Green, aka "Mistress Ivey," prescribing chastity usage in her *KeyHolder's Handbook—A Woman's Guide to Male Chastity and Sexual Teasing*. The time-honored chastity belt, historically used as a rape-prevention device or to discourage childhood masturbation, it turns out, is now a vital part of BDSM role-play. As the *Huffington Post* reported, CB-X, the "world leader in male chastity," now sells the lockable sheaths in wood, chrome, and camouflage finishes.

So oversexed are we that even good, God-fearing Christian women are aping porn stars. Out on the Web, a sect of gals calling themselves "Christian Nymphos" have taken to exploring, graphically, the fine points of marital relations and the connubial sacrament. I hear where they're coming from, though as a Christian myself, I prefer not to spiritualize sex, even when playing Wayward Priest and Naughty Nun with the missus. The last thing I want to think about, as the Christian Nymphos do, is to "ask the Father to give you the heart of the Shulamite Woman (for Him and for your husband)."

But the Christian Nymphos go on, like most oversharing habitués of the Internet, getting into the literal ins-and-outs of every position from "The Pile Driver" to "The Italian Chandelier." I don't presume to speak for God, but by the time He gets to their spiritual forum on anal plugs, I suspect He'll be regretting the divine grace of sex and wishing He'd settled for a gift card to Bed Bath & Beyond.

So oversexed have we become that even some secularists have decided to take matters in hand, so to speak. A popular subsite on the user-based aggregator Reddit is "No Fap," where "fapstronauts" take the "Fapstinence Challenge," attempting to shake their porn and masturbation addictions through total abstinence from both. Its organizers cite all manner of incentives to participate, from increasing self-control to freeing up hard drive space. ("Some porn collections can take up terabytes of information.")

Fapstronauts, of course, are easy to make sport of. And yet, it's a little harder to laugh at the fact that there are now over eighty thousand of them on this one little website. You don't have to be a chastity champion or antiporn activist to recognize that something is seriously out-of-whack in the culture. I like sex as much as the next guy. But it's getting strange out there. Our appetites increasingly know no bounds, running the gamut from dendrophilia (erotic interest in trees) to oculolinctus (a sexual urge to lick the eyeballs) to toxophilia (arousal from archery). Americans will do *anything* these days—and we've got nothing on the Japanese.

An acquaintance of mine, Ron Fuegobutt, says, "When sex is too indiscriminate, you don't even enjoy it anymore." At a dinner not long ago, he was seated next to the retired porn star Ron Jeremy, who is the John Gielgud of the genre. By Jeremy's own estimate, he's had sex with a good four thousand women on film. "He explained to me," Fuegobutt says, "that after all those years in porn, he can still get it up, but he can no longer finish. He's like Sisyphus—the task is never completed. It's horrible."

With so many of the stigmas gone, so, too, are many of the thrills. As it is written in Proverbs, "Stolen waters are sweet, and bread eaten in secret is pleasant." But good luck finding a secret place anymore. In our orgiastic pursuit of instant gratification, few mysteries are left. All of our appetites are known and celebrated and unrestrained. Want to see a man love up on a tree? A two-second Google search will show you images you can never unsee.

All this thinking about chastity—and tree huggers—had me turn to a priest friend. His porn-star generator name is Father Chuck Looselips. He holds that people are mistaken, getting intimidated by thinking of chastity as something that has to be taken as far as the Mother Church requires him to take his. Instead, Father Looselips says that we should think of it as a worldview, as balance, as just enough. "In a culture of obese, depressed people with attention deficit disorder, we know what *too much* does." What does *just enough* look like when we apply it throughout our lives: "How much do you eat? How many televisions do you watch at the same time? How many people are you talking to simultaneously? We are overdoing it to our own destruction. We lose the sense of taste, the sense of appreciation, the sense of pleasure. How do we break this cycle? By a 'less is more' philosophy. By balance. By just enough."

Everyone and everything, says Father Looselips, "has a chance for excellence." But to attain it, we have to observe laws. The laws of our creation. "A chair is excellent if the wood is hard enough to hold a person. If it obeys the laws of gravity. If the seat is horizontal to the earth and is cut to the contours of the butt. All of this requires obedience on the part of the carpenter. Obedience to wood. Obedience to gravity. Obedience to comfort. It requires obedience to laws we did not create, and the smarts of knowing what these are through discovery."

The same, he holds, applies to sex. How much truer this is of people than chairs. In regard to chastity, he says, "It means less is more, just enough, just right, the right person, the right time, the right closeness, and the right distance, and no more than that."

For the married, that means, "I strive to be the best friend, the best lover, the best husband and father, with the family we create." This is a tall order, he concedes. "Human life is messy. We are neither angel nor devil (usually), but we have both influences and need to balance them all the time. Life is a long tightrope walk between two skyscrapers. Modernity is a constant consumer and has no use for the idea that less is more. It has no concept of *just enough*. And we are seriously suffering on every level—physical, emotional, psychological, mental, and spiritual—from our own excesses. But we are all better off knowing the obedience that is required to live healthy and excellent lives."

Without these principles, we're not really living at all. We trade the beautiful expectancy of Christmas Eve for the per-petual anticlimax of Christmas morning. We lose mystery and wonder. We fail to cultivate and appreciate. We hunt for con-stant novelty, failing to rest in the fullness of our own passions. We are no longer making the simple, beautiful music of man/ woman song, with its harmonies and melodies and rhythms. We're not even making an atonal loveless racket, the racket Paul described, in his letter to the Corinthians, as that of a sounding brass or tinkling cymbal. Instead, no matter how much sex we're having, we as a culture are making a lonely, sad, muted sound. The sound of one hand fapping.

CHAPTER 10

Simplicity

Or, the Many-Splendored Virtues of Hoarding

James Lileks

I NEVER GOT THE CHANCE to ask Aunt Beulah about the hatchet in the wall. In the photo she's sitting in a chair, looking pensive at something off-camera, and you can't tell if she's mad at the person who just spoiled a perfectly good wall by chucking a tomahawk into the plaster or whether it had been there for years and she's bothered over a remark her sister made about the drapes. *It's just like her to say that. Really, she always has to say something.* The rest of the wall is empty; perhaps they took all the pictures down when the party got plenty hot and someone wanted to play Ed Ames. I don't know.

Nor did I ever ask Aunt Edna why she posed for a shot on a small-town street in the late 1940s. Neon signs for EATS and hooch; gleaming black cars hunched along the curb like hunkering beetles. She's standing stiff with her arms at her side, a sunny smile with a squint. A Kodak for a beau overseas, maybe. A memento of a trip into town: *Here I am in Hot Springs!*

It's impossible to ask, since they're not my real aunts.

I've no idea who these women are, actually. I met them at the antique store I visit now and again. They always have a shipment of orphaned photos for sale, hundreds of tiny pictures ripped from books, the soft, black scrapbook paper still stuck to their backs. "Fifty cents each!" said the sign. *Instant family!* I thought.

I figured I'd pick up a few amusing shots. That was at the beginning. It's something of a habit now. I always wonder about the people who bring the pictures into the store. What are they thinking? *Oh, it was Grandma's photo album, she's long gone.* Or, *Mom died, and we have no idea who these people are.* Or, *What can I get for it?*

The scorn of your ancestors, that's what you'll get. But it's a relief when the history passes from your hands, I suppose: These strangers aren't your responsibility anymore. The people in the small, overexposed pictures look out as if they know you, but page after page of rangy men outside of barns, farm women in the yard holding bonneted baby blobs, interchangeable farm dogs, uniformed brothers back from basic—it doesn't mean anything. Which is one way of saying it just means too much. Out it goes.

The best ones get snapped up by people who have the time and temperament to sift through the history of strangers. As much as Beulah may have hated that axe in the wall, it bought her a ticket away from the flame.

"Real photos": That's what they're called in the ephemera trade. I don't collect them, but I have some. There are people who collect phone cards; I'm not one of them either, but I have some of them, too. In fact I may have the world's most complete collection of Sprint 1992 Presidential Phone Cards. They were handing them out at the GOP convention, and I wheedled a set out of a PR person. It's likely that 90 percent of them were pocketed and forgotten. They fit in a cassette-tape box. They'll make someone happy some day—but not in the first-kiss sense, not in the great-meal sense. The fleeting and solitary pleasure of acquisition and completion. As far as I know, the cards still work, which gives them a potency you'd spoil by squandering the minutes on an actual call. A collector would want to know if they'd been sullied by use.

So the phone cards go in my closet, waiting for whomever. When I come across them periodically, they remind me of something else. In the GOP convention merchandise hall I bought a ticket from the 1892 GOP convention in Minneapolis, my adopted home. A ticket for the press. Beautiful engraving, minor wear, twenty bucks: Sold. (I don't collect tickets, but I have a few.)

Go forward ten years; my dad is getting ready to move from the house where I grew up, and we're going through the drawers. Manila envelopes of things Mom saved. Grandma's farm diary from the 1930s and '40s. (Laconic to a fault: weather, condition of the crops, social notes. I kept hoping I'd find "Helen Gunderson came over with laudanum, day spent in fairyland." But no.) Bank books from institutions long-ago gathered into great impersonal conglomerates. Newspaper clippings Dad saved because he was the subject of the story: Father and son enlist on the same day; local fuel-oil truck struck at intersection; fire consumes loading dock at West Fargo station; local man catches robbers.

Eh? Sure enough: Here's a clipping from the *Fargo Forum* detailing how a local businessman, concerned about pilfering at his warehouse, waited in the office with an employee and loaded shotguns. Check the date: Mom's home on a hot July night, eight months along with me. The thieves showed up for a third night running—Dad hits the lights and walks out and KABOOM—fires one off overhead to lay down the plot for the rest of the evening. One of the crooks runs the odds and drops right there; the other flees. When his confederate gives him up, the cops go to his house, where his wife insists, "He's nowhere, sir, haven't seen him all night." Dirty boot-prints lead to the closet. Off he goes.

What a tale! I flip open the laptop, Google the names: One of the miscreants went on to a life of petty crime—and his son was killed by his wife and her lover for the insurance money decades later. I'm stunned. *You never told us about this,* I tell Dad.

He smiled. Never came up, I guess.

Can I have this clipping? Sure.

I don't collect newspapers, but I have a few. My thinking went like this: At some point the entire paper's archives will be digitized, and this yellowed, flaking scrap will be redundant, but there's a difference between looking at a piece of scanned microfilm on a screen and holding in your hand the article cut out by the wife who was proud of her husband even though he could have gotten himself killed. I set it aside and looked at the next item in the stack.

It's an 1892 Minneapolis convention ticket. Identical to the one I bought ten years before, except that it's a visitor's pass. My great-grandfather had attended. This was the sole proof of his trip, which, I knew, ended at a train station in Minneapolis that no longer exists. Yet I visit that part of town from time to time; I walk where he walked. I got married on an island in the Mississippi close to the place where the convention was held. I work for the newspaper whose office would have been one of the buildings he saw when he left the station.

Can I have this ticket? Shrug. Sure.

The two tickets sit side by side on my shelf in the closet where I keep the things that matter. I know what they mean, separately and together. I'm the link between the two. I gave meaning to the objects that they couldn't express on their own. I have explained this meaning to my daughter.

"These are somewhat valuable, and they are family heirlooms, which is why after I'm gone I want them to go the historical society, because otherwise a jittery boyfriend with rings in his ears and tattoos will make you sell them to get money for his demo record. Really, I would have thought you could see through him."

"Dad. Please."

"I'm just telling you now. They're pieces of history that belong with appreciative curators, and I need to know you're not going to be standing there while the boyfriend asks the pawnshop manager what he can get for them. He's going to think they're worth a lot because they're old, but really, forty bucks, tops. You don't want to get that sick feeling that you're selling off your dad's collection to make your boyfriend happy, and that feeling ought to tell you he's not right for you."

"Does your valuable collection include the Starbucks cards?"

"That's *completely different.*"

Sigh. I don't particularly like Starbucks. I have no interest in plastic-card collection. But these cards are commonplace ephemeral objects, the daily detritus, discarded because they're numerous and have no value once the numbers have been logged into a smartphone app or spent in a store. But someone will want them, someday.

"That's *hoarding,*" she says. Well, it's not hoarding if the cards are in shoebox #14 on the shelf in the closet, okay? I have three thousand matchbooks because someone, somewhere, set them aside. There's a website devoted to old candy wrappers that shows us the style of bygone candy because someone set them aside. I couldn't care less about gift cards, but someone will. It's not hoarding. It's philanthropy.

Also, it's for you, my child.

In the basement, under the stairs, there's a plastic box with plastic bags, numbered by year. Disney tickets, Happy Meal toys, plastic wristbands from the place where we went on winter days when she was four. Someday, if she wishes, she can hold her childhood in her hands, and imagine the events that made me set these things aside.

And then sell them.

Because my daughter grew up in the digital world, every *Proustian* madeleine is a series of ones and zeros on a frangible platter. Her creations are literary and artistic; she has written a novel, made movies and animations. And as she grows she disavows everything she's done before. She'd trash the lot if she ever cleaned out her computer. She has no idea that every so often I peek at her computer, find the best work, and print it off. She has no idea that I have saved our text messages in a long scrolling file of quotidian conversation. It may mean nothing some day, and I don't blame her if she discovers the cache of memory and sighs with annoyance: *What I am supposed to do with this, exactly?*

That's the question, isn't it?

Sometime around 1997 a New Yorker died and left some cufflinks from the World's Fair, and the kids went through the drawers, sighing, wondering why Dad kept all this junk. They had no idea that he bought the cufflinks because he'd had the best day of the summer with a pretty girl from up the block who hadn't given him a thought until he got that job at Alexander's and fixed himself up right with a new suit and sharp shoes. When he asked her to go to the Fair she said *Why not?* to herself and "Why not?" to her girlfriends. "It's not like he's so hard to look at." They took the subway. They saw the robot who smoked cigarettes. They went to the Wonder Bread pavilion and had samples. They ate at the Swiss Restaurant. They walked along the lagoon at sunset and watched the fireworks and she gave his hand a squeeze, and he was over the moon. When they were waiting for the subway he saw a stand that had souvenirs and bought her a hair-clasp with the Hemisphere and Peristyle, and she said he should get those cufflinks, too. They were smart.

Handshake and a cheek-smooch on the Brooklyn stoop. He went home and threw the cufflinks in the drawer and never wore them. Now and then when he went through the drawer he'd come across them, and wonder who would wear those things today, the Fair all gone and forgotten. *Huh. Who was that girl? Frances.* He'd pick them up and look at them and remember her legs and her smile and think, *Ahh, she wasn't for me.* But he never told his wife about her. A guy'd be crazy to do that.

And so they ended up on a table in a parking garage on a Sunday and I bought them.

Note to future matchbook historians who wonder how a foil-covered matchbox from Haugen's Ice Cream Parlor in north Fargo survived from 1976: I dated a cheerleader in high school. Briefly. She wanted to meet there to give me the heave-ho. The waitress asked what she would like to order, and she declined. "This won't take long," she said. I pocketed the box on the way out. In those days you helped yourself to matchbooks when you left. If the meal was bad it wasn't a total loss.

I'd collected matchbooks for a while, but that was the first time I took one because my heart was broken. It makes me wonder if every matchbook I have from someone else's collection was saved for the same reason.

The matchbooks from childhood were stored in old Butter-Nut coffee cans. I use them now to hold backup DVDs of writing, photos, and . . . well, scans of matchbooks and plastic cards. Can't toss them: This is what Butter-Nut looked like in 1972.

A few of these must still survive, filled with screws in Dad's workshop, or treasured in a collection of vintage cans. This one happens to hold the bytes that describe my life in the years after my mother died. There's just no way she could have known when she reached for the can at the SuperValu one morning that it would sit in a closet in the impossible year of 2014, holding the digits that described the granddaughter she never met. I have no idea what my mother was thinking at the time, or worrying about, or whether Paul Harvey was on the radio thundering about Head Red Brezhnev the moment the opener bit into the soft metal, the pressure escaping with a fragrant whoosh. It's possible forensic technology could pull her prints off the can.

If someone offered me ten bucks for it tomorrow, he could have it.

Too much meaningless meaning, really. *It's just a can.* If it needs an intermediary to explain its importance, best to let it go and stand on its own merits.

That's the hard part of trawling through the antique store; nothing has an advocate anymore, and the story starts fresh when you buy it and take it home. *Sometimes.* I found a drawer of old love letters from the forties, neatly typed on government stationery. I took a seat, Googled the names, and came up with their obits. Bought 'em, scanned 'em, put 'em up on the Web. One of the letters had place cards from a dinner the couple attended before they were married. She saved them for a reason.

I had to screen-cap the obits, though. They'll drop off into the limbo of 404 eventually. Same with my site with the matches and family photos, of course, but you can only hope it gets scraped by some dispassionate automated harvesting mechanism. So the couple's love letters float on and on until they unravel in the churn of expired domains and sundered page links. It would be hoarding to keep the letters; it would be folly to think anyone who went through my stuff someday would care.

On the next trip to the antique store, I put the ones I'd bought back in the drawer with the rest.

Nearly everything I've collected in the last twenty years I could sell tomorrow. Once I've scanned it, it's dead weight. I love the heft of the old *Life* magazines, solid and pliable as a seal's flippers, and I'd sell them off except that someone would cut them up and sell the ads. Fifteen years ago coming across a cache of *Life* in an antique store was like stubbing your toe on a pirate's chest; now the entire run has been digitized and put up for free by Google. For collectors it's like being an old man in a spaceship that took decades to reach another star system, and when you get there you find it's been colonized by people who invented light-speed drive a few months ago. The worthless currency of foreign lands, the matchbooks, the postcards— the objects themselves mean little. The scanned versions that reside in the cloud of the Internet mean more: By researching the stories behind the images as best as I can, they have a tale to tell again.

An admission: If the house were on fire, it wouldn't be the postcards or magazines I saved first. It would be a few items from the shelf in the closet where the remnants of middle-period childhood sit. A pink plastic drinking glass the Welcome Wagon brought when we moved into our new rambler; it was the hated receptacle for the Warm Salt-Water Gargle prescribed by Dr. Mom when we had a sore throat. And a spy-pen that had a built-in microscope. (Up to 2X!) A vial of gun oil for my Daisy

BB rifle. Membership cards for the Cub Scouts, the Fargo Public Library, the Merry Marvel Marching Society. Items from the sweet spot of childhood . . .

And my grandmother's hat-pin box. I didn't know it was from the 1893 Columbian Exposition until I took Brasso to its tarnished finish. Inside is a thin ribbon of gold, which was removed from the bridgework of my great-grandfather after his death. My daughter thinks this is *TOTALLY DISGUSTING*. But I put the box in her hand and say: You're holding something from a man who fought for the Union. He lay on the battleground left for dead, but got up, healed, headed north, and split the sod. He is the reason we're here.

Everything can go in the cloud but that. Over this gold his breath passed, his words moved.

A few years back in Fargo I found a scrapbook that belonged to Doris, the woman my father married after my mother died. They grew up in the same rural community, so many of the characters that appeared in my mother's scrapbooks showed up in Doris's account of North Dakota in the 1940s. But she'd been an import, brought to the prairie after the war. The book had pictures of childhood and one stood out: a squinting little baby on the steps of a Brooklyn brownstone with a concrete planter on the stoop. I asked Doris if she remembered where she lived, and she did; a few keystrokes on the laptop to call up the address on Google Street View—and there it was.

The planter was still on the steps, seven decades later.

I should have bookmarked it. I should have copied the picture and sent it to the people who lived there now. I should have done my part to weld the tiny image from the FDR days to the twenty-first century. But it doesn't really matter. The look on Doris's face when we found her childhood home on the computer was all the story needed to end. Now and again, tinder and flint meet, and that's enough.

Simplicity is a virtue, but it's often misunderstood. People take it to mean that *stuff* doesn't matter. We tell ourselves that it's virtuous to divest, lest we become hoarders. The thing about hoarders, though, is that they think they'll need their stuff someday. They have it backward. The *stuff* needs us to tell their stories. Just once. Before they pass along to the next set of hands.

The things we save are nuggets in a sieve, and when our hand falls from the handle they tumble into the river again. But for a while you can handle the physical object and conjure its story.

CHAPTER 11

Thrift
The Un-American Virtue

Joe Queenan

AMERICANS LIKE TO THINK of society as the individual household writ large. This is especially true when they are in an ornery mood.

"I can keep my financial house in order," they argue. "So why can't the federal government?"

Well, the federal government *can't* keep its financial house in order. It just can't. It tried once or twice over the years, but things didn't work out. It can't keep its financial house in order because society is not, in fact, the individual household writ large. And society's attitude toward the virtue of thrift proves it. Thrift—usually defined as the wise management of one's finances, occasionally bordering on frugality—is reasonably common at the micro level, where individuals and families and even entire regions of a country may practice it on an intermittent, if highly selective, basis. But with few exceptions, the virtue of thrift is not practiced at the national level. Certainly not in this country. Not recently, at least.

You can make the case that the Scots are thrifty, and the Swiss, and perhaps *ze* Germans, but you could not say the same for the French, the Spanish, the Italians, the Brazilians, the Russians, the Saudis, or the Chinese, much less for the farcical societies that abound in the third world. In their defense, most societies are not in a position to be thrifty. Thrift is a concept that denotes volition on the part of the practitioner; it is not merely an instinctive, knee-jerk response to adverse economic conditions. Poor, third-world countries are never actively frugal, not in the sense that they consciously practice frugality as a virtue. They are frugal because they don't have any money. The words "destitute" and "frugal" are not synonyms. Nor are the words "flat-out busted" and "thrifty." It should not be necessary to explain this.

On these shores, the public's attitude toward thrift is more nuanced. Backed into a corner, at least some Americans would probably identify faith, hope, and charity as virtues. They might even give a grudging nod to humility, in the sense that they view the practice of humility as a virtue in the abstract, without aspiring to being humble themselves. No, the closest Americans ever come to being humble is when they are polite. Americans do not believe that the meek will inherit the earth. They believe that Americans will inherit the earth. (The numbers seem to be in their favor.)

Vis-à-vis chastity, qua virtue, a great number of Americans would be on the fence, in their chicken suits, as they would be with the puzzling, largely discredited, and now virtually obsolete virtue of temperance. Patience would be a nonstarter in this rambunctiously impetuous society. Ditto thrift. For as long as anyone can remember, Americans as a people have behaved in a bellicosely unthrifty fashion, spending money as if it were going out of style, as if there were no tomorrow. No, I suspect that most Americans are not even familiar with the concept of thrift while others simply abhor it. If forced to take a polygraph, I dare say our countrymen would refuse to identify thrift as a virtue. They might even deem it a vice. In a society that depends so heavily on the consumers' purchasing power, the thrifty are sometimes viewed as quislings, spoilsports, turncoats, renegades, goldbricks, party poopers, enemies of the republic.

The American economy, the most powerful-yet-mysterious engine in the history of the world, is built around the idea of inducing lots and lots of people—both at home and abroad—to buy lots of stuff they don't need, in order to create lots of jobs for other people, who will then buy lots of stuff they don't need either. There is no room for thrift in such a pitiless (though generally rather entertaining) Leviathan. The concept of thrift derives from the maxim, "Waste not, want not." But Americans do not honor this maxim. To them it sounds contrived and inane. To them it is a hoary anachronism, like "A penny saved is a penny earned," or "It is better to light one candle than to curse the darkness." Which is to say, it is a colorful Ben Franklinism with no relevance to contemporary life. "Waste not, want not" resembles *Honni soit qui mal y pense* or *Dieu et mon droit*, pithy expressions from our glorious past that no longer resonate in this grasping, fun-loving society.

Economists are endlessly wrestling with the idea of thrift. In their view, a properly functioning economy must strike a balance between savings and debt. If people are utter spendthrifts and buy more things than they can possibly pay for, then society will eventually run aground. This is what happened recently to the Irish, the Greeks, the Spanish, and the Portuguese, all of which are voluptuously clownish societies. In each case, the public's eyes were bigger than their stomachs. And now they (or at least *ze* Germans) will pay the piper.

But if people are too thrifty, spend too little, and keep too tight a clasp on the purse strings, a society can also run into problems. This is what happened in Japan over the past quarter-century, where the locals would enthusiastically produce fantastic cars and televisions to be sold overseas, but would not buy any of these attractive, lifestyle-enhancing items themselves.

They would work their fingers to the bone to bring a ray of sunshine into the lives of anonymous foreigners, while languishing in the technological tar pits themselves. This sort of behavior often leads to drink. Thrift carried to such lengths becomes a vice, a faux pas, or at the very least, a deplorable habit.

What are the characteristics of thrifty people? Basically, the thrifty are the kind of loners who like to hunker down, batten the hatches, take a breather, sit this one out. They lead lives of quiet, but relatively inexpensive, desperation. They honestly enjoy this sort of stuff. They are voluntary outcasts at life's rich feast. To paraphrase the immortal Santayana, one of those luminaries who is only famous for saying one thing, those who cannot remember hunkering down in the past are condemned to hunker down in the future.

Thrift, unlike, say, honesty or charity or perseverance, is a virtue that goes in and out of fashion. Whenever the economy craters and the Four Horsemen of the Fiscal Apocalypse begin to canter across the horizon, pundits start gasbagging about hitting the reset button and returning to "our core values." Our lost values. Our forgotten values. But this is stupid. Our core values *are* spending money and buying stuff we don't need. The entire hemisphere was discovered by rapacious conquistadors and cash-strapped sea dogs on the prowl for the lost cities of gold. It wasn't the Little Sisters of the Poor who landed at San Salvador, much less at Jamestown.

In short, this society hasn't saved its way to greatness. It spent its way to greatness. It is a society that started maxing out its credit card even before credit cards were a gleam in Mr. Visa's eye—and enjoyed every second of it. In doing so, we have merely imitated the Roman Empire, the only society to which our own can be fairly compared, for both good and ill. Two thousand years of overspending was the way the Romans did things, and not a single regret. No, when pundits say, "We need to hit the reset button," what they're really saying is, "We need to go back to living like the Puritans or the Shakers. Or like me and my wife, who grew up in a dirt-poor hamlet in rural Vermont and were perfectly happy to make do with frayed hand-me-downs until the age of fifty." Nobody in this society really wants to hit the reset button—nobody but the pundits and a few isolated naysayers and harbingers of doom. Hitting the reset button isn't any fun. Nothing that pundits suggest is *ever* any fun.

In essence, thrift is a virtue that resembles being very good at mah-jongg. You've heard about people who can do it, but you've never actually met any of them. The *campesinos* say that the thrifty are in the hills or the mountains or the lost arroyos or the snow-capped *barrancas* and will only return when the people desperately need them. In other words, the first Tuesday after never. Thrift is a virtue that people have heard about but have never seen practiced. "They do it over there, but they don't do it here," David Bowie once sang, referring to fashion, though thrift would have been just as good a target. You may have a maiden aunt who is renowned for her thriftiness, or perhaps an economy-minded distant cousin who was last heard from at a garage sale in Newfoundland in 1973. But you don't know any thrifty people at the local level. Nor would you wish to. They would only tell you to turn down the thermostat and eat more day-old bread.

Even when thrifty people appear in our midst, they tend to keep a low profile. This is because the thrifty are always worried about being confused with the cheap. The cheap person is the guy who goes to an expensive restaurant with friends and orders the priciest thing on the menu and then refuses to pay his fair share of the bill. The cheap guy says, "I only had a spritzer, not the chianti." The cheapskate always stiffs the waitress. The thrifty person is not like this. The thrifty person is tight, but he is not evil. The thrifty person always pays his fair share of the bill when he goes out, but he never goes out. The thrifty avoid proximate occasions of extravagance by staying indoors. Cheap people are repulsive, whereas thrifty people are merely annoying.

By the same token, thrift must not be confused with miserliness or avarice or penury. Thrifty people are by no means perfidious. Thrift and cheapness are not interchangeable. Cheap people are skinflints and tightwads and chiselers and swine. Misers are scum. They spoil things for everybody. Thrifty people, admittedly, can get on your nerves, but not to the point where you start to hate them. The pathologically cheap, by contrast, make you want to garrote them with piano wire.

Thrifty people only buy things at the right price. They are born with an internal calculator that enables them to arrive at the correct price for any product or service. This is usually 30 percent off the previously discounted price of 50 percent off. Misers, by contrast, don't care what price you put on an object. Misers don't buy things.

Thrift, like chastity, is technically an acceptable virtue, so long as not everyone practices it. If everyone were chaste, the human race would be much, much smaller and a lot less fun, and Las Vegas would cease to exist. If everyone were thrifty and made do with old clothes and old cars, there would be no jobs for people who made new cars and new clothes, and the economy would quickly grind to a halt. Thrifty people know how to indulge whims in an inexpensive fashion. The thrifty person may overpay for premium ice cream, but he will not overpay for a hotel in Glasgow. He will pay to eat candy at the multiplex, but he will never buy his candy at the multiplex. He will bring his own candy, by God.

Thrift is not a one-size-fits-all virtue. There are various kinds of thrift, as thrift is not practiced at all times and all places in equal measures. There is *actuarial thrift*, the pathological need to set aside money for a rainy day, even when one knows full well that no such rainy day will ever arrive. This is the sort of grinding, soul-destroying thrift practiced by well-heeled retirees who worry that their money will run out if they live to 112. (And also by the English.)

Then there is *ostentatious thrift*, the chronic need to show off the bargains one has recently acquired, even though nobody else cares. *Preening thrift* is practiced by wealthy people who drive hybrid cars not because of the gas mileage but because they like to make neighbors feel guilty about driving morally indefensible gas-guzzlers. This is also called *double-whammy thrift*, an opportunity to show others that one is both virtuous and thrifty. *Pedagogical thrift* is the sort of thrift that is used to instruct and even torment the young. "You can have a toy, but only if the toy costs less than ten dollars. And if you break the toy, I will not replace it. Ever." Pedagogical thrift often borders on *punitive thrift*: "You left your tennis racket out in the rain, so now you will have to go to Rutgers instead of Princeton. I hope that teaches you a lesson."

This brings us to the curious case of *autumnal thrift*. This is the sort of thrift that is practiced as the gloom begins to gather around the gloaming, as the Grim Reaper's melodramatic approaching footsteps can be heard sauntering up the driveway. In 1992 my wife and I purchased a Toyota Previa van that lasted eighteen years and 169,000 miles. Last year we purchased a Toyota Camry. I am now sixty-three years of age. I hope to live to be eighty, but only if I am lucky. If the Camry lasts as long as the Previa—and there is no reason to believe that it will not, given that I no longer have teenagers racking up huge mileage on the vehicle—it could be the last car I ever buy. Every single time I get into that car I am aware that I am driving what could be the last car in my life.

That's why I never drive it. I let my wife drive it. Currently, I have a nine-year-old minivan, and I hope that it lasts another five years. But after that I'm going to start leasing a new car every three years, just so I will not be oppressed by the thought that the vehicle I am tooling around in could be my last compact sedan before the darkness. This is a clear case where thrift gets depressing.

For the most part, thrift does not quite coalesce with our national skill set. Some people would even argue that thrift, carried to excess, is a threat to our national well-being. That said, the intermittent practice of thrift is not to be deplored. Thrift is like fasting—an activity that helps tone the emotional muscles and prepare one for the future, should dark times appear. Thriftiness is a virtue to be held in reserve in case it is needed in times of crisis. People should be capable of acting in a thrifty fashion, should the need to tighten the purse strings ever arise. Thrift is a laudable virtue, in its way, but one that should only be used in emergencies. It's a bit like playing the banjo: a little goes a long, long way.

CHAPTER 12

Honesty

It's Absolutely the Best Policy (Sometimes)

Rita Koganzon

IN 2010 A HARVARD SENIOR named Adam Wheeler applied for a Rhodes scholarship with amazing credentials. In addition to his perfect GPA, he'd won Harvard's senior thesis prize as a junior, coauthored four academic books—with two of his own under way—lectured on seventeenth-century English poetry and Zoroastrian cosmology, and knew such improbable languages as Classical Armenian and Old Persian. Instead of spending the following year at Oxford, however, Wheeler spent it in prison. Nearly everything on his résumé had been invented, forged, or plagiarized, down to his admission to Harvard, which was based on doctored SAT scores and fake transcripts from schools he'd never attended.

Wheeler's was not the first such case. In 2008 a similar run of forgery and imposture was discovered at Yale. In 2007 a woman spent nearly a year at Stanford masquerading as a student. In 2006 another woman borrowed the identity of a missing person to attend Columbia after having attended Harvard under a different false identity. Such incidents have occurred with predictable regularity since the darkest antiquity, which is to say, since at least the 1980s, shortly after competition for elite university spots became a national obsession.

Self-invention and imposture are, of course, hardly the discovery of Ivy League aspirants. In open societies, wherever credentials bestow honor and fame, someone will inevitably be prepared to fake them. Where there is no Ivy League, no Wall Street, no Silicon Valley, other channels for rapid upward mobility and repute will be found. In 1704, for example, there appeared in London the first native of Formosa (modern-day Taiwan) whom Londoners had ever met, a certain George Psalmanazar. The English, captivated by his bizarre manners and exotic tales, encouraged Psalmanazar to write a book explaining the grotesque customs of his native land. All this brought him considerable renown, but, as it happened, George Psalmanazar was actually a destitute Frenchman who'd never been in the vicinity of Formosa and knew no Asiatic languages. Everything about his persona was an elaborate fabrication, down to the ingenious claim—advanced to deflect questions about his distinctly European appearance—that his pallor was the result of the Formosan tradition of living underground. Remarkably, the discovery of Psalmanazar's charade did him little damage; he went on to a moderately successful career as a writer and scholar, one that likely would not have been possible had he not caught London's attention with his Formosan tales in the first place.

Should Psalmanazar have suffered for his self-misrepresentation? Putting aside what he was not, what Psalmanazar turned out to be was a gifted linguist and a respectable scholar in need of patronage and exposure. His deceit was, we might say, a victimless crime. True, readers who bought his book thinking it a true account of Formosa were duped out of their shillings, just as Harvard was bilked out of several thousand dollars in scholarship and prize money by Wheeler. But to count the wages of such deception in purely monetary terms misses the point. As a canny character in Herman Melville's *The Confidence-*

Man observes about such frauds, "Money, you think, is the sole motive to pains and hazard, deception and deviltry, in this world. How much money did the devil make by gulling Eve?"

People like Psalmanazar and Wheeler aren't interested in stealing fortunes or taking lives, but in getting an unearned share of esteem and prestige from society's supply, earned shares of which are often disbursed according to dubious principles of merit anyway. So what good is honesty? As a virtue, it's clearly a sometimes thing. When we all know that "the system" can be gamed, why shouldn't we applaud the most audacious players—or better yet, join them?

To some degree, all ambitious college applicants are junior varsity Adam Wheelers. Everyone knows what admissions committees want to hear—that they were born without money, parents, or a majority of their limbs; that they rescued abandoned puppies, attended to pediatric cancer patients, and tutored a moderately sized village in sub-Saharan Africa, all while holding down an A average and playing goalie for the state-championship soccer team. College admissions has become an elaborate game of exaggeration and self-promotion not wholly unlike outright self-invention. One impressed writer for the student gossip blog *IvyGate* put the dilemma clearly:

> The loquacious and devious Adam Wheeler presents us with quite a pickle. He's learned our language, mastered our ways, and taken the self-promotion and ambition that we're all groomed for—yes, all—to its natural conclusion. . . . If it walks like an Ivy student, talks like an Ivy student, then it is, without a doubt, an Ivy student.

Imitation can be as good as the real thing, when the real thing is itself bankrupt. If impostors like Wheeler can slip past the exalted gatekeepers so easily, then what's so special about the stuff behind the gates? Very little, according to David Samuels's 2008 book, *The Runner*, an account of serial con man James Hogue's 1989 effort to win admission to Princeton by inventing the persona of a self-educated cowboy orphan who "read Plato under the stars." Although Hogue's application was a wholesale fabrication, once at Princeton he proved a stellar student, earning nearly all As. By contrast, Walter Kirn, who attended Princeton the "honest" way a few years before Hogue, explained his approach to his studies thusly:

> I relied on my gift for mimicking authority figures and playing back to them their own ideas disguised as conclusions that I'd reached myself. . . . I sought solace in the company of other frauds (we seemed to recognize one another instantly), and together we refined our acts. . . . I came to suspect that certain professors were on to us, and I wondered if they, too, were actors. In classroom discussions, and even when grading essays, they seemed to favor us over the hard workers, whose patient, sedimentary study habits were ill adapted, I concluded, to the new world of antic postmodernism that I had mastered almost without effort. To thinkers of this school, great literature was a con, and I—a born con man who hadn't read any great literature and was looking for any excuse not to—was eager to agree with them.

When it's frauds all the way down, past even the turtles, what possible justification is there for the ambitious to develop those "patient, sedimentary study habits" that will win them nothing but Bs and a slow, painstaking rise to middle management?

Kirn can afford to admit all this to us now, three decades after the fact, precisely because these youthful tricks resulted in a highly successful writing career. Would you, too, like a successful writing career? Talent in the arts is hard to quantify and subject to variations in taste. Every step after college admission requires ever more aggressive self-aggrandizement. Everyone's doing it. So what does it hurt to improve your self-presentation a little? As long you don't find yourself going by a fake name.

Or at least not more than one at a time.

That's the line the opponents of honesty trot out, anyway. They emphasize that the system is full of holes, that its most successful products are self-inventors of a sort only barely discernible from the outright frauds, and that the best response to all this rottenness is to be even more rotten than everyone else. Either because nothing less will get you where you want to be, or because the spread of rot will speed the collapse of an already hollow structure.

There is, to be sure, another view. The Impostor Defense Front is checked by what we might call the Honesty Enforcement Front. Honesty enforcers respond to the same provocations by doubling their commitment to "the system," and trying to seal the cracks in the structure through which Adam Wheelers slip. It's hard to know who's worse.

For every Adam Wheeler who wins a seat at Harvard, the members of the Honesty Enforcement Front argue, twenty honest, hard-working, high-achieving, never-sleeping applicants are left out in the cold. (And one of those just happens to be their very own child!) All of which is why admissions offices ought to conduct top-secret, clearance-level background checks on applicants. And if schools aren't going to tap into the NSA's records, then at least there ought to be a test for such things.

One test, for the whole country, everyone sitting for it at the same time, and felony convictions for cheaters. It could be like just like China's *gaokao*.

Like the Impostor Defense Front, with its mixed constituency of sincere strivers looking for an open door and hardened cynics looking to bring down the edifice, the Honesty Enforcement Front is also an uneasy marriage of opposites. There are the hard-line panopticists, who would not let a single lie go undetected. These have made common cause with preachers of the gospel of authenticity, another parent-heavy sect that believes that poor Adam Wheeler was driven to his misdeeds by the intense pressure and competitiveness of our society, which prevents students from "just being themselves" or "learning for its own sake." If only we didn't push ourselves and our children so hard! Once we're freed from competitive impulses, our authentic selves will emerge from encrusted layers of self-promoting spin. As totalitarian as a panoptic world of enforced honesty might sound, it's hard to know if it's really worse than this alternative world in which nothing is worth lying about because there is nothing to strive after.

Against both the Impostor Defenders and Honesty Enforcers, we might consider how the particular dishonesty of imposture is, like obesity, an unsightly sign of a certain kind of societal health—and one whose natural punishments are sufficient to put us off imposing artificially draconian measures against it. As our faux-Formosan friend demonstrated, the phenomenon of self-invention is neither uniquely American nor uniquely contemporary, and our Adam Wheelers are perhaps best understood in a context broader and wider than the woes of the modern American university or its diseased appendage, the meritocracy. Imposture is an inevitable result of open and mobile societies. It is the dark side of free markets and free movement. Adam Wheeler isn't a symbol of American social immobility. Just the opposite. It is precisely because a kid from a public school in Nowheresville *can* get into Harvard that Wheeler tried to do so.

But it is also *because* Wheeler could get into Harvard by fraud that public school students everywhere can continue to do it honestly. Melville wryly observed that the suppression of barbarous forms of criminality like brigandage "would seem cause for unalloyed gratulation, and is such to all except those who think that in new countries, where the wolves are killed off, the foxes increase." Rather than signaling civilization's decay, fraud grows out of security, prosperity, and above all, trust. It is opportunity's cost.

Precisely because the line between self-improvement and self-invention is so elusive, honesty is difficult to value properly. Benjamin Franklin, the first and perhaps greatest of America's self-inventors, conspicuously left honesty out of his catalog of virtues. Instead, he preferred "sincerity," which he defined "us[ing] no *hurtful* deceit"—a definition that leaves ample latitude for ambition's designs. Franklin saw clearly the demands that a commercial economy and democratic sociability would make on us, and strict honesty was not among them.

Fortunately, self-invention has a certain natural limit in the very sociability that spawns it. We undertake to improve ourselves—even to the extent of outright self-fabrication—in order to win the esteem of people we aspire to be like and to befriend. Yet friendship requires us to sustain consistent identities, to be trustworthy and reliable, while successful fraud requires quite the opposite—a constantly changing identity whose foundations no one can know. The highest pleasures of friendship—its intimacy and confidence—are the very things the self-inventing fraud must avoid at all costs. The perfectly undetectable fraud may be doomed to perfect loneliness. This is a higher price for success than most strivers are willing to pay.

This is, admittedly, all a rather sanguine view of the self-limiting nature of fraudulence, and the necessity of tolerating even the most preposterously deceitful cases of it. It would be remiss, even *dishonest*, to omit the darker view of the situation depicted by Melville, which is perhaps the definitive account of the price of American self-invention. *The Confidence-Man* follows a protean figure aboard a Mississippi steamboat who spends an April Fool's Day convincing the boat's cynical passengers to invest their "confidence," and usually a small monetary deposit, with him. The boat is a microcosm of the reigning spirit of the country, "the dashing and all-fusing spirit of the West, whose type is the Mississippi itself, which, uniting the streams of the most distant and opposite zones, pours them along, helter-skelter, in one cosmopolitan and confident tide."

This spirit is animated from one end by the hard-boiled suspiciousness and self-reliance of a frontier people, embodied in the attitude of the boat's barber, who hangs a "No Trust" sign from his door. But from the other end, it is fed by an exuberant faith in all the faddish indications of man's moral progress— nature, science, markets, even the idea of "moral progress" itself—that threaten the frontier man's steady distrustfulness, mainly because these were always the optimistic motives for conquering the frontier in the first place. The boat's passengers boast of their practiced skepticism upon meeting the confidence-man, but he quickly discerns what it is that they do believe in, and they become opportunistic philistines under his spell, serially felled by his indefatigable exhortations to trust in the goodness of man. This is a dim picture of America—

incorrigibly gullible, vulgar, greedy, self-immolating. Indeed, *The Confidence-Man* has often been read as an indictment of the easygoing commercial American disposition drawn for us by Franklin, and the character of the confidence-man (not incorrectly) taken for a distinctly American Satan.

But *The Confidence-Man* is, in the end, a satire, even if it is a satire of a fallen world inhabited by the devil. The comic vacuity of the confidence-man's "philanthropy" and his victims' ridiculous pretensions to misanthropy show us the pettiness of both our desire to succeed through deceit and, just as importantly, our outrage at finding ourselves the victims of such tricks. Melville picks up the Hobbesian insight that nothing pricks our pride more, "nothing triggers a stronger impulse to hurt someone," than to be made a fool.

If occasionally misplaced trust is unavoidable in a porous, commercial society like ours, then we ought to be wary of both the Impostor Defenders and the Honesty Enforcers. Just as our first impulse when watching a confidence trick unfold is to envy the confidence man, our first impulse at being duped by him is to demand traps so pervasive and effective that no one can ever elude them. But the satisfaction of such impulses would require undermining the very openness and mobility that make our liberty possible, all for the sake of thwarting future George Psalmanazars and Adam Wheelers.

The strongest argument against such folly is to realize how utterly absurd these charades are, how inveterately stupid we are to fall for them each time—and how frankly funny this fact is. Melville warns that indulging in illusory visions of moral progress weakens our defenses against fraud. Our evidently incurable susceptibility to even the most preposterous lies is his evidence that moral perfection is in fact illusory. Just as perfectly reasonable and even highly educated people mistook an obvious Frenchman for a Taiwanese refugee, so did equally reasonable and highly educated people believe that an obscure college junior had compiled the academic résumé of a senior Harvard professor.

This is our comic lot, stuck as we are between perfect knowledge and perfect depravity. We must "suspect first and know next," as one of Melville's passengers confidently asserts, but we can't suspect all the time, or know everything. Since we are for the most part too credulous and too sociable to either beat 'em or join 'em, our best hope is to expect them, and to moderate our outraged humiliation when they, predictably, appear. It's safe to assume that our reason will reliably continue to fail us— our boss's degree from the South Pacific University of Erehwon will prove to be fake, and our neighbor's blood relationship to the crown prince of Denmark will turn out to be fractional descent from Danish peasants. It's good to be wary. But it's also good to consider that too much suspicion erodes honesty as effectively as too much trust. It is good, too, to remember that gullibility is the flip side of charity, and we are fortunate to have the luxury of credulousness.

Fraudulent self-invention is an old road to success, but a narrower and more potholed one than many of those seeking to either direct traffic to it or close it off understand. Even those who avoid exposure along the way find that, at its end, there is no one with whom to share their success. Having duped everyone else, their reward is the esteem and exclusive company of fellow impostors. Those seeking a lonely life of endless evasion for a dinner date with those whose greatest achievement is claiming someone else's achievement are unlikely to be diverted from their course by exhortations to virtue. But the high road is sunnier, wider, and better paved. And it draws the better travelers, among whom it's easier to find someone who'll lend you a buck after you've been bilked.

CHAPTER 13

Fellowship

Reach Out and Touch Someone

Christine Rosen

IF YOU GREW UP among the Protestant faithful, as I did, your church probably had something called Fellowship Hall. A large meeting room separate from the main sanctuary, Fellowship Hall featured lots of worn vinyl chairs and a bad sound system and was used for everything from teen youth group meetings to senior aerobics. It carried the distinct smells of canned gravy and good feeling.

But Fellowship Hall was also the physical embodiment of a misunderstood virtue. The Greek word for fellowship, *koinonia*, suggests camaraderie, commitment, and bonds with others. The word appears often in the Bible. In the Christian tradition, believers are encouraged to form fellowships with the likeminded faithful and to avoid fellowship with unbelievers. (And devils. Fraternization with them is looked down on, too.) Fellowship is valuable because it's something to be carefully entered into, and then cultivated. We might choose our friends, but when you join a fellowship, you are signing on for something more than the mere pleasure of another's company. You're joining a group with obligations, responsibilities, and an implied duty to the other fellows.

In this sense fellowship has always suggested a more serious commitment than friendship. It requires willingness to weather life's challenges side by side with your comrades. Although the word itself is gender neutral, it has a distinctly masculine vibe—men create fellowships (Jesus and His apostles; the Bee Gees); women create covens. The word also conjures ragtag bands of people thrown together under less-than-ideal circumstances, say, the quest to throw a magic ring into a volcano while being pursued by marauding orcs. You know the sort of thing. Your fellows are the people who look out for you no matter the cost to their own safety and lives, and you do the same for them. Even when they're hobbits.

And yet fellowship has a desultory pedigree in America. Despite the frequency with which our presidents condescend to their "fellow Americans" in speeches, the word lacks any real civic power. Harding was the only president to mention fellowship in an inaugural address, and he did so with an obsequiousness more suited to a dating website than the leader of a great nation: "We sense the call of the human heart for fellowship, fraternity, and cooperation," he said in 1921. "We crave friendship and harbor no hate." Mencken likened this pap to "a string of wet sponges."

In a nation that has towns with names such as Hell (Michigan), Squabbletown (California), and Comfort (Tennessee), as far as I know there is only one place named Fellowship. It's a small, unincorporated town in central Florida. In stark contrast to the Walt Disney World Industrial Complex nearby, the town of Fellowship appears to embody the ideal of a small community, with a commons situated near the town's Hog Pond and lots of churches. (It's also number 79 out of the Top 101 U.S. cities in terms of highest average humidity, which is notable primarily because it means that on this list, Fellowship charmingly outranks Hell.) Perhaps some of that small-town fellowship in Fellowship will spread to its close neighbor, Ocala, a city whose motto—"God Be with Us"—suggests a peculiar municipal anxiety. Then again, Ocala, which is known for its bucolic horse farms, also happens to be home to "The Funking Conservatory," a full-service professional wrestling school—no, I don't know what that means, either. But conservatory graduates include a fellow named "Chris the Bambi Killer," so how bad could the place be?

If you don't find fellowship in the names of many towns, you see it invoked all the time in the names of "senior living centers." (This euphemism for nursing homes is a gift from the aging baby boom generation, which insists on the pretense that old age is merely a vigorous new life stage rather than a parade of horribles leading to the undiscovered country.)

There's something unnerving about the forced cheerfulness of retirement communities. Take the Fellowship Senior Living Center in Basking Ridge, New Jersey. On the center's website, amid Photoshopped images of spry octogenarians cavorting on well-manicured lawns, is the reminder: "You'll Value Our Wonderful Way of Life." The unspoken part of the message is obviously: *Or else.* Although clearly meant to imply friendly camaraderie during one's golden years, the use of the word "fellowship" in this context feels strained, like watching Brad Pitt trying to do Ibsen.

Why is our view of fellowship so ambivalent? Probably because it's a virtue that can be put to good uses, or ill. Sure, Bands of Brothers vanquished the Nazis. But Richard Nixon's paranoid "palace guard" were all equally devoted to their cause. For every cuddly Von Trapp family singing their way out of danger, there's a Kardashian clan scheming to marry off their daughters for the benefit of reality television. These are all fellowships, of a sort.

It's time to restore fellowship to its rightful place among the virtues. In fact, it's essential, because we need *something* to replace "friendship," a word that has been so adulterated by social media that it makes the Real Housewives look like Vestal Virgins. Grumpy old people (that is, anyone over the age of thirty *not* currently pursuing a retrosexual relationship with an old high-school flame they found on Facebook) will remember those halcyon days when the word "friend" did not have scare quotes around it. When you weren't expected to like. Or pin. Or retweet. Or +1 everything that everyone you have ever known regurgitated onto the Internet.

Of course, much of social media's appeal lies in its low barrier to entry for friendship. As my grandmother used to say about politicians, I have heels higher than their standards. Facebook, for instance, allows you to manage friendship the way you manage your bank account: Withdraw when you feel like it, deposit new people into the fund, or reconcile accounts by blocking people you really don't want to hear from. This can be useful when an acquaintance wants to regale you with the details of his latest juice cleanse. But it encourages a corrosive form of multitasking that allows us to indulge in the sanctimonious *feeling of* having cared and tended to our friends when what we've really been doing is scanning our Facebook page while binge-watching *Game of Thrones.* As for Twitter, it dispenses with the pretense of sentiment entirely. Like Jim Jones with his Kool-Aid, you simply have "followers" who, if they know what's good for them, retweet everything you say.

As a result, social media encourages a kind of socialist view of friendship, both by the leveling effect it has on all of our relationships and by a diabolically efficient method of redistributing attention in the form of likes and retweets. And it never stops. Open your Facebook page after a brief hiatus and you feel like a goose experiencing *gavage.* The metrics are brutally transparent. You didn't retweet your friend's pithy observations on craft beer or like your acquaintance's latest pictures of her adorable toddler? By the debased standards of the Internet, *this* is what makes you a horrible friend.

The technology-enabled form of compulsory fellowship has taken a toll on society. After years of wading through status updates and Instagrammed meals and aspirational Pinterest collages, friendship now seems like a kind of virtual corporate retreat where we're forced to do one trust-building exercise after another. Add to that the false sense of familiarity we culti-vate about the lives of others—particularly public figures—and you've critically weakened the foundations for true friendship. The entertainment industry inundates us with so many details about celebrities' (and would-be celebrities') lives that it's now possible to know more about the grooming habits of your favor-ite starlet than your best friend's dream of opening an artis-anal pickle shop (coincidentally, both involve elaborate brining rituals).

What we need is a new kind of fellowship, not the vapid kinship suggested by President Harding or the shared senescence of the senior rest home. We need a fellowship based on something so simple and retrograde that it's practically heretical: physical interaction. Think of it as a fellowship linked to sociality, which is only achieved when we are in close proximity to others (like the disciples packed in for a Last Supper, not the contestants locked away on the ranch on *The Biggest Loser*). Think of it this way: sociality is to social media as meditation is to crack cocaine. Or as actual sex is to pornography.

A fellowship grounded in sociality means enjoying the com-pany of those with whom you actually share physical space rather than those with whom you regularly and enthusiastically exchange cat videos. Proximity defines many of the enduring friendships we find in myth, literature, and history: Achilles and Patroclus, the above-mentioned apostles, Jeeves and Wooster.

And this kind of fellowship is a reassertion of an older form of group behavior—the fellowship of those who met regularly at the café or pub, or the fellowship of the knitting circle. Today we have followers, flash mobs, and supposedly wise crowds, all of which are said to be an improvement on the old days. But the "fellowship" we have with other people in the digital world is of an overly involved and emotionally volatile type. It's the manic camaraderie of the pop-star fan-page message board, or the trending hashtag, or the flame war. And it's an ultimately weak attachment precisely because it never manifests in the physical world.

Of course social media isn't entirely to blame for debasing friendship. Long before Facebook and Twitter, frenemies reveled in each other's weaknesses and mistakes. (By the by, why hasn't someone created an antisocial networking site called SchadenfreudeBook? I'm just saying.) As Bertrand Russell once observed, "Nobody ever gossips about other people's secret virtues." Even people who belong to a fellowship of shared interests and passions can't always resist the basest human impulses. Consider writers. When an aspiring poet sent "Ode to Posterity" to Voltaire, the old Jacobin is said to have replied, "I do not think this poem will reach its destination." William Faulkner once said that Henry James was "one of the nicest old ladies I ever met." After listening to Oscar Wilde charm an otherwise adoring American audience, Ambrose Bierce peevishly declared him a "dunghill he-hen" prone to an "opulence of twaddle."

But if the weaknesses of fellowship are a permanent part of the human condition, technology has exacerbated the problem. And soon our technologies will know more about us than we would ever be willing to admit to someone else. Big Data knows your secret passion for the German power ballads of David Hasselhoff and the extent of your narcissistic self-Googling habit. How many of us would be honest enough to confess this to our friends? And how many of our friendships in turn rely on the little white lies we feed our friends? "We'd *love* for your toddler triplets to join us for the wine tasting!" "No, no—go ahead and text during lunch. I'm sure it's important." "Of course a woman your age can wear that dress!" I prefer the honesty of a friend who once sent me an e-card that read, "You're the friend I'd feel the worst about killing in a postapocalyptic death match for food."

What to do? Let's return to Fellowship Hall—or at least the ideal of Fellowship Hall. (What the world needs now is *not* another staging of *Joseph and the Amazing Technicolor Dreamcoat*.)

Fellowship requires the real presence of others, not an audience of untold millions. Technology has offered opportunities for connection we have never had before—though we somehow survived in the days before we were able to talk to random (often naked) strangers on Chat Roulette. It has probably also helped us avoid dealing directly with acquaintances whose views we don't share. It's easier to ignore annoying tweets and status updates than it is to sit across a table listening to the inanity of someone we know. But it is the challenge of in-person fellowship that is also its strength, and real fellowship is not the same thing as membership in the compulsory mutual admiration society often fostered by social media.

Sometimes we need to show up for the people who need us. And we need to know when to stop performing our friendships online. (Unlike the Hoff, who once told an interviewer, "The problem with me is that nothing embarrasses me.") Fellowship, like old-fashioned friendship, involves risk, and not just the risk of having an embarrassing photo uploaded to a friend's

Facebook page. It is the risk of revealing ourselves to another human being and having that person reject us, or laugh at us, or simply ignore our efforts to connect. But without risk there is no reward—the possibility of finding a kindred spirit, an intellectual sparring partner, or an ally during that postapocalyptic death match for food.

We increasingly live amid the ether of the cloud and the pixelations of the screen, forgetting that our greatest tools for communicating with each other as human beings are not our sleek smartphones and laptop computers, but our less-than-perfect faces, gestures, and voices, even when we are at our most annoying. (What do you mean you don't want to learn more about my farm-to-table, zero-carbon, raw-food vegan lifestyle?) It is only when we are face-to-face and physically present with one another that we can experience the kind of genuine fellowship that has been the hallmark of civilization. In a world of digitally debased "friendship," that is a virtue worth prizing and practicing rather than merely retweeting.

CHAPTER 14

Forbearance
Opting Out of the Politicized Life
Sonny Bunch

NOT SO LONG AGO, in an op-ed for the *Los Angeles Times*, a woman by the name of Madeline Janis spent 751 words of precious editorial-page real estate bemoaning the fact that she didn't like her dying father's politics. Miss Janis, a progressive lioness, wrote that her dad routinely refused to engage her in arguments. Instead, he preferred enjoying her company and talking about less contentious topics. Yet while moving him into an assisted-living facility, she came across his dark secret. The villain owned a collection of Rush Limbaugh hats. Janis told her father he should throw them out.

"Rush Limbaugh is nasty and mean-spirited," she hectored. "Can't you at least stop wearing these caps?" When he said no —after all, why should his daughter care which ball cap he wore?—the two went to their separate corners. Some time later, Janis's father came to her and said that his love for her eclipsed even his partiality for Limbaugh. Since the hats were causing her so much distress, he tossed them. The truly odd part of the story is that to Janis, her badgering of an old man represented, somehow, a lesson in tolerance.

"Our love for each other and our family helped my father and me transcend the enormous ideological divide between us," she wrote, without apparent irony. By "transcend" she probably meant "traverse," with all of the movement coming from her father; "tolerance" really meaning the capitulation of the other side.

The left doesn't have a monopoly on political monomania, of course. The libertarian writer and activist Eric Dondero ostentatiously promised to cleave all Democrats from his life following the reelection of Barack Obama in 2012. He envisioned his *cri de coeur* not as a protest but as a plan of action: If everyone cut the Democratic cancers out of their lives, he argued, then we might save this once-great nation.

"I strongly urge all other libertarians to do the same," he wrote. "Are you married to someone who voted for Obama, have a girlfriend who voted 'O'. [sic] Divorce them. Break up with them without haste. Vow not to attend family functions, Thanksgiving dinner or Christmas for example, if there will be any family members in attendance who are Democrats."

Dondero's Lysistrata act went further—much further—than just crossing his ankles until the Democrats were out of the White House. "Everybody I know that voted for Obama is dead to me," Dondero told the *Washington Times*. "I don't want to talk to them again. I don't want to see them again. I won't even attend their funeral. The nation committed suicide November 6." On the one hand, at least Dondero didn't pretend that his righteous fury was an act of reconciliation and understanding. On the other, it was disturbing to hear such pure rage vented in the public square. Would Dondero really refuse to visit a dying Democratic relative in the hospital, as he told *New York* magazine? Is that what the world is really coming to?

As the kids say: Well, duh. Just take a look around.

The antidote to this poisonous view of the world is forbearance. Forbearance allows us to ignore perceived slights and to carry on about our business. I say "perceived" because most such slights are just that. Janis's father, for instance, probably wasn't holding on to his Rush Limbaugh hats just to tweak his daughter. And Dondero's Democratic friends and relatives probably weren't voting for Barack Obama just to cheese him off.

But in a world without forbearance, a perceived slight is just as bad as a real one. And as we have ushered in the age of the politicized life, forbearance has been pushed hastily to the side.

What's the politicized life? It's the growing, pernicious trend in American society where politics are injected into every moment of one's existence. Stories of the politicized life bubble up almost daily. When it became public that Chick-fil-A's executives oppose gay marriage, there emerged, overnight, a mass movement to boycott the restaurant. When the man who founded Whole Foods dared to posit that Obamacare might have suboptimal outcomes, people huffily responded by declaring they would get their kale and quinoa elsewhere. Thirty years ago, Orson Scott Card wrote a classic science-fiction novel called *Ender's Game.* Just recently, the book was made into a movie. But in the intervening years, Card had the temerity to say that he thought gay marriage might create problems for society. So our high-minded elites instituted a boycott on the filmed adaptation of his book—and this only after having him blacklisted from other writing projects.

The Internet exacerbates the politicized life to an almost cartoonish degree. There are people—and even big-money-backed corporate websites—who dedicate themselves to finding grievances. These malcontents spread their angst like a plague: Every disagreement and every microaggression offers an opportunity to display their righteousness.

For those who haven't spent much time around racial studies departments on college campuses, a "microaggression" is something a "privileged" person accidentally does to a "marginalized" person to make them uncomfortable. ("Privileged" is normally just code for "white males," but it's a sliding scale.

Recently, even the feminist left has cried out about the thought-less aggressions of privileged radical feminists against marginalized radical feminists. Go figure.) For some context: The politicized feel that asking a person of Asian descent whence he came—that is, where his ancestors came from—is a horribly offensive thing to do, a "microaggression." The reductio ad absurdum of the genre may have occurred in late 2013 when a group of minority doctoral candidates complained that a UCLA professor was a serial microaggressor for highlighting typos in doctoral dissertations. No, really. Evidently, pointing out improper semicolon usage is now the highest form of racism.

Anyway, once you've been aggrieved by some microaggression, the retweets and Facebook likes take care of the rest. The more outrage you generate, the more applause you earn. It is not a system conducive to contemplation or thoughtful discourse. It's charming to recall that, once upon a time, people thought that the Internet was terrible because the only things people used it for were looking for at porn and posting pictures of their cats. Oh, to return to those golden days.

The Internet—along with its slow-witted progeny, social media—helps groups of like-minded individuals coalesce into little communities of the righteous, where they are constantly trying to outdo one another with displays of outrage. It's a perpetual motion machine of anger. And these instant coalitions of fellow travelers render forbearance obsolete. In real life, you forbear those around you because you never know who thinks what, and forbearance makes it easier for the whole neighborhood to get along. There is diversity of thought, in part because no one really cares what the guy who lives next door thinks about marginal tax rates. But in virtual life, everyone in the self-selected group pretty much thinks the same thing, about everything. And the occasional deviations become opportunities to enforce the communal norms, to show how super serial we all are about the righteousness of whichever cause binds the community together. While tolerating (nay, embracing!) diversity of race is one of the few remaining secular virtues—one not to be questioned, at any time, by anyone—tolerating diversity of opinion has become a rare beast indeed.

In George Orwell's *1984*, the "Two Minutes Hate" is a regularly scheduled occurrence in the state of Oceania. During the Hate, all good party members are required to stand before a television screen and scream obscenities at a parade of ideological enemies. The book's protagonist, Winston, is as ambivalent about the ritual as he is about the society in which he lives. However, even he is powerless to resist the crowd's passions as the state-mandated shrieking reaches its crescendo. "The horrible thing about the Two Minutes Hate was not that one was obliged to take part. On the contrary, that it was impossible to avoid joining in. Within thirty seconds any pretense was always unnecessary."

The Two Minutes Hate is real today. Here's how it works: An enemy is identified, a crime is announced, and vitriol spews forth. The specifics of the crime don't really matter. It could be someone saying something nasty—or just unpleasant, or even suspiciously nice—about a protected group. It could be a business executive donating to an outré cause. All that matters is that we are presented with a face to hate. But our Two Minutes Hate is actually worse than Orwell's, because (1) it's not directed at constructs like "Eurasia" and (2) the government doesn't orchestrate it. No, the modern Two Minutes Hate is directed at living, breathing people. And its targets are designated by a spontaneously created mob—one that, due to its hive-mind nature, is virtually impossible to call off.

Consider the case of literary agent Sharlene Martin. Martin

represented a juror from the George Zimmerman trial who was shopping a book about her experience. Tensions were high following the case, which had ended with the acquittal of Zimmerman in the shooting death of the black teenager Trayvon Martin. The mob fixed, for no discernable reason, on Sharlene Martin.

"You are a [*sic*] bottom-feeding scum, which is perhaps tautological for agents," read one aggrieved tweet.

"Bitch u better not publish that book," read another.

"You are a total waste of life."

"YOU ARE CLEARLY RACIST."

You get the idea. One enterprising member of the mob discovered Martin's office address and phone number and published them. Her place of business was flooded with harassing phone calls and emails. Threats were made against her and her workplace. She was berated for hours on Twitter before deactivating her account and retreating from the world of social media entirely.

Or consider the case of Justine Sacco, a flack for Barry Diller's IAC who, before boarding a flight bound for Africa, tweeted, "Going to Africa. Hope I don't get AIDS. Just kidding. I'm white!" While the merits of her joke are debatable, the response was swift and vicious. After a website highlighted her missive it was picked up by the mob at large. White-hot anger spewed forth. "An apology can not fix what you have said ma'am. The kill yourself section is to the left. Have a good day," said one aggrieved party. "I hope you trip on a flat surface, fall, have a ride over you, die, go to hell and get analy rape! [*sic*] Racist bitch!" wrote one well-wisher. Within hours the hashtag #HasJustineLandedYet was born. You could practically see a Twitter mob, larded up with digital pitchforks and torches, waiting for her to land in South Africa. She was promptly fired, which sated the mob's bloodlust. For a few hours, anyway.

There are little explosions like this every day on the Web. Sometimes the target is famous. Sometimes it's just an ordinary person who happens to have attracted the notice of the pack by cruel chance. In an interconnected world, where more and more people are living the politicized life, there are always targets. Someone is always thinking the wrong thing or saying something disagreeable.

The question is why, when someone says something disagreeable, can't people stop themselves from disagreeing? Part of the answer might be the rise of social media, which appears to be increasing impulsivity among its users. Research from Keith Wilcox of Columbia University and Andrew T. Stephen of the University of Pittsburgh suggests that increased use of social media can lead to a host of deleterious effects. "Findings showed that more time spent on Facebook was linked with a higher body mass index, increased binge eating, a lower credit score, and higher levels of credit card debt," as the *New York Daily News* summarized the findings. The commonality, of course, being diminished impulse control. Spend enough time on social media and, literally, you *can't* help yourself.

Impulsivity is the mortal enemy of forbearance. Forbearance calls on us to sit back and reflect on our behavior, to consider our actions and those of others in context, and, in turn, to engage the world in a reasonable way—often by bearing disagreement with grace and good humor. The Internet, on the other hand, encourages the opposite. It asks us to act quickly and snarkily, with self-assurance and in a manner pleasing to our self-selected followers and friends.

One of the most unsettling aspects of the politicized life is that those who embrace it are not un-self-aware. They know what they're doing and they believe it is right, just, and necessary.

Impulsivity is no vice for the self-righteous. And for the self-righteous, forbearance is no virtue. After all, these people are trying to fix the social order! And the sooner they can fix it the better. Patience? That's for the privileged. "Be patient" is what the powerful tell the marginalized to keep them quiet. As the bumper sticker says, "Well-behaved women rarely make history." And bumper stickers are never wrong. (You might even think of them as the ancient progenitors of Twitter.)

In recent years we've been besieged by sociologists and political scientists claiming that polarization in America is on the rise. They're no doubt correct. And there is some evidence to suggest that the Internet is, at least partially, to blame. The 2012 American National Election Study, for instance, found that the number of people who describe themselves as "liberal" or "conservative" had ticked up by three points from the previous cycle. But this study was conducted in two formats—one where it asked people questions face-to-face and another where it asked them online. And in the online version, polarization was far more pronounced.

What does this mean? Well, for starters, it means that we're more likely to indulge in hyperpartisanship when staring at a computer screen than when we're confronted with a real, live human being. But what does *that* mean? Are we simply being more honest with the screen? Or does the act of parking in front of a monitor prime us for hyperpartisanship? Or is the very nature of online interaction changing how we behave and how we think?

No one knows for sure, of course. I tend to suspect that selection biases—that is, choosing to read only things we agree with and choosing to interact only with those with whom we agree—combined with the immediacy with which we can consume news and deliver our opinions to the world, has fundamentally altered the way we behave. And not for the better.

There's nothing wrong with talking politics, as Madeline

Janis did with her father. In fact, we owe it to the Founders (and ourselves) to stay informed and aware of the world around us. By the same token, there's nothing wrong with standing up for your beliefs and attempting to persuade those with whom you disagree. But there's a difference between having polite, rational discussions and declaring those with opposing views to be the enemy and, therefore, worthy of destruction, infamy, and impoverishment. Consider, for example, how difficult it would be to tweet the *Federalist Papers*, which are the platonic ideal of political persuasion. (Or, if you really want to despair, ask yourself if the *Federalist Papers* could be written in the age of Twitter.)

All of that said, until our robot masters take over the world, the Internet isn't going away. So what our polity needs is a bit more forbearance. A good bit of it. Accept that people who vote differently don't want to destroy the republic. When someone you know says something wacky, don't argue with them— try smiling, being pleasantly bemused, and moving on in the conversation. (This goes double when the wackiness comes from someone you don't know. First of all, you're not going to change their mind. And second, why do you care what they think?) But above all, the next time a Two Minutes Hate ramps up, step away from your computer and get a cup of coffee. You'll be a better person. And you'll feel better, too.

Forbearance is the rare virtue that provides its own rewards.

CHAPTER 15

Integrity

Living by the Code of the Superman

Jonah Goldberg

THE OXFORD ENGLISH DICTIONARY defines "integrity" in part as "soundness of moral principle; the character of uncorrupted virtue, esp. in relation to truth and fair dealing; uprightness, honesty, sincerity." This is basically what most of us have in mind when asked to define "integrity." A man of "great integrity" is a man who is honest, forthright, and incorruptible. In the secular faith that is Americanism, George "I cannot tell a lie" Washington is about as good an exemplar of the idea as one can conjure.

Then again, that's what we're supposed to say. It's a bit like when pollsters ask people, "What is your biggest concern?" No one says, "The San Diego Chargers beat the spread this weekend," or "I think I got the clap from that waitress." But surely that sort of thing is closer to the truth for most people. I live in Washington, and while lots of people say their biggest concern is "the deficit," I have yet to meet anyone who has lost sleep over it. Regardless, certain answers are expected of us, and so people say things like "entitlement spending" or "the plight of the uninsured." We say that because it's the sort of thing we want to believe about ourselves. We want to believe that we're good people.

That's one of the interesting things about integrity, according to the moral philosophers (at least the good ones). Integrity in the moral sense isn't defined simply by *doing* the right thing, but by *wanting* to do the right thing. Philosopher Harry Frankfurt laid out a hierarchy of desires. Every animal has the thought, "I want to have sex." Many animals—mostly the better ones—might have something like the thought, "I want to reproduce." Only humans think: "I want to marry a nice Jewish girl who'd make a good mother." Badgers don't think to themselves, "I must crush all of my enemies so I can rule supreme as the emperor of the North Woods and have my choice of the finest badger sows to copulate with." It is the desire to have moral or immoral desires and the decision to act upon them that defines humanity at its best. Integrity is the measure—or at least one important measure—of how successful we are at acting on our desire to have the right desires.

David Thunder (the Irish philosopher, not the American porn star; I think) identifies five types of integrity, but I won't burden you with the full list; it's not going to be on the test. Suffice it to say, the five kinds of integrity are really just a spectrum. At one end, there are "purely formal accounts of integrity," according to Thunder (I wish he were more strident so I could write "Thunder thunders"). "Somebody may be committed to evil causes or principles, and they may adopt principles of expediency or even exempt themselves from moral rules when the rules stand in the way of their desires." At the other end of the spectrum are "fully substantive accounts." In this version, a person with integrity is someone "who desires to do what is morally good in all of his decisions."

There was a time when this desire-to-do-good-in-all-things was considered the *only* kind of integrity. After God Himself, the exemplars of integrity are the angels, who are God's intermediaries to the physical world (at least according to Maimonides and the producers of the old CBS series *Touched by an Angel*). Angels are better than mortals. They're always certain about what is right because, by definition, they're doing God's will. (As no one says, "If it's from the Almighty, it's alrighty.") Gabriel knew when it was okay to remove a mattress tag and Sandalphon always tipped the correct amount.

Meanwhile, humans are like Hong Kong knockoffs of angels, in that we have a divine spark in us, but sometimes it goes dim when Cinemax After Dark is on. As Psalm 8 says, "For thou hast made him a little lower than the angels, and hast crowned him with glory and honor." Free will means that we can fall short of doing the right thing. As James Madison put it, "If men were angels, we wouldn't need the IRS criminal enforcement division." (I'm paraphrasing.)

Still below angels, but above normal men, are heroes. Traditionally these are people who do the right thing at great personal sacrifice. The Greek *hērōs* means protector or defender. Sometimes protectors must do bad things for the greater good. Knights, at least as a mythic ideal, strove to be as close to angels as humans could be. In the later Middle Ages, the angelic ideal of chivalry was democratized as the bourgeois sought to raise their children according to gentlemanly rules of honor, too. Even as the chivalric code evolved, the idea of heroism remained largely intact. Heroes make sacrifices for the greater good. Tom Doniphon, the man who actually shot Liberty Valance (spoiler alert!), cut some corners, but he did so for a higher good. The incorruptible Dirty Harry was dirty in a legalistic sense, but closer to the angels in his desire for divine justice. (Angels in the Hebrew Bible never read the wicked their *Miranda* rights and weren't exactly above opening a can of whoop-ass when necessary.)

But something in the culture has changed. Throughout virtually the entire history of Western civilization, heroes had the right-end-of-the-spectrum version of integrity. They did good out of a desire to do good—and that good was directed by some external ideal. Sure, it wasn't always, strictly speaking, a biblical definition of good. You can't blame Odysseus or Achilles for not following a book that hadn't been published yet. But however "good" was defined, it existed in some sort of Platonic realm outside of the protagonist's own Id. (Or ego? Or super ego? Or super-duper id? I can never keep that stuff straight.) The hero clung to a definition of good that was outside of himself, and therefore something he had to reach for. Not any more. Now everyone reaches inward for their own vision of integrity. Or, as Omar Little says in *The Wire*, "A man['s] got to have a code."

In case you didn't know, Omar was arguably the most popular character on the critically acclaimed HBO series about inner-city Baltimore. As a gay murderer who stuck to robbing and murdering drug dealers, Omar was what passed for a man of integrity in the show. Ditto for Walter White, the main character in AMC's wonderful series *Breaking Bad*. White was a chemistry teacher turned drug kingpin and mass murderer. The show's creator, Vince Gilligan, explained that the idea for the show was to turn "Mr. Chips into Scarface." Gilligan succeeded, but not before he seduced and corrupted the viewing audience, too: By the time the story ended, fans no longer minded that Walter White had become a homicidal drug dealer. They rooted for him anyway.

While the audience could forgive White's murdering and drug peddling, they couldn't abide the fact that his (fictional) wife wasn't more supportive of his (fictional) career choice. Facebook pages, blog posts, chat rooms, and other algae plumes of the digital ocean expressed outrage and hatred for White's wife, who insisted, as best she could, that issues of right and wrong trumped her husband's vanity. It got to the point where the actress (Anna Gunn) who portrayed the poor, beleaguered Mrs. White wrote an op-ed for the *New York Times* complaining about the tsunami of hate aimed at her character, which had spilled on to her in real life as well. In liberal pop culture this was the equivalent of yelling "I'm telling!" and running to the principal's office.

Gunn blamed the whole thing on sexism. Her complaint may have some marginal merit, but it's also really, really, really boring. The more interesting explanation (i.e., *my* explanation) is that "purely formal" integrity is really the only kind of integrity our culture celebrates anymore. Superman—who always does the right thing—is blah. Batman, a vigilante who plays by his own rules, is sexy.

Speaking of Superman, Jerry Siegel, the cocreator of the character, first used the term "Superman" to describe the villain in his 1933 short story, "The Reign of the Superman." The character was based on Nietzsche's *übermensch*, the man who breaks from the herd to create his own set of values independent from an (allegedly) dead God. To Nietzsche, reason and traditional morality were for squares. Siegel and his partner, Joe Shuster, quickly abandoned the evil, *übermensch-y*, Superman idea and instead turned the character into a classic hero—a protector who personified the highest form of substantive integrity. They repackaged the make-your-own rules *übermensch* a few issues later as the villain Lex Luthor.

And that might be where they went wrong—because Nietzsche has clearly won the popular culture. I get that talking about Nietzsche and the popular culture—or really Nietzsche and anything—is like reading Proust during the time-outs at a Packers game in Green Bay; it assaults the nostrils with the scent of the poseur.

So, as Joe Biden's intelligence briefers like to say, let me simplify the point (albeit without the use of the VPOTUS hand puppets). When I talk of the triumph of Nietzsche, all I mean is that do-it-yourself morality, informed by personal passion rather than old-fogey morality, is the new norm.

One of my favorite guilty TV pleasures is the series *Banshee*. The show's premise isn't particularly important for the purposes of our discussion, but suffice it to say my inner twelve-year-old boy finds all of the nudity and violence totally integral to the plot. In one episode there's an Eastern Orthodox priest—who is also a Ukrainian mob boss, naturally—who explains that ultimately every man is beholden to a code he creates for himself. (This was shortly before he took out a machine gun and sprayed bullets at his own niece, in his own church.) Now, contrary to popular misconception, I am not an expert on the theology of Byzantine Christianity and its flowering in Ukraine. But I'm pretty sure this not an accurate treatment of church dogma.

I bring up the Ukrainian priest/capo not so much because it's a good example of what I am getting at—in this case, at least the character was a villain—but rather to note that once you become aware of the movement to define integrity as a commitment to self-made principles (no matter how evil), you see it everywhere you look in the popular culture. We've already touched on *Breaking Bad*. There's also the TV series *Dexter*, in which an avowed psychopath/serial killer adheres to an ethical code that he actually labels "The Code." It's his own personal rulebook, which says that it's okay to murder—with psychosexual delight, even—so long as the people you are murdering are also murderers. That might sound like a modern adaptation of old-school morality, except it doesn't take long for Dexter to cut himself some slack and start killing innocent, but inconvenient, people as well.

Remember the heroes of *The Sopranos*? They were all murderers and thieves who justified and rationalized their crimes on the fly, too. In one episode, Paulie "Walnuts" Gualtieri and Christopher Moltisanti killed an angry waiter they had stiffed on the tip. And afterward they learned an important lesson: not to let work interfere with their friendship. Who is *Mad Men*'s Don Draper? He's a narcissist raised in a brothel who treats his personal vanity as if it were the chivalric code. Then of course there is Frank Underwood, the protagonist of Netflix's remake of *House of Cards*. Underwood has no code to speak of, save that everything and anything is justified if it increases his political power. It's hard to exaggerate either the popularity of the show inside the Beltway or how little Washingtonians care that the show's hero is irredeemably evil.

Admittedly, many of these examples come from high-middle-brow fare and pay cable. But teenagers and kids are getting the same messages, too; they just need to have the idea pounded into them a bit more directly. Take the wholesome-sounding movie *The Girl Next Door*, which plays on basic cable channels with a constancy normally reserved for documentaries about Kim Jong-un on North Korean TV. Matthew Kidman, the nerdy protagonist, is a teenage boy who falls in love with a porn star who's moved, well, next door. All his life poor Matthew's been a do-gooder who does what is expected of him. He's a substantive-integrity kind of guy. In a speech contest for a college scholarship, he's expected to talk about "Moral Fiber." But that was before he fell in love with his neighbor, who has—through a series of fortunate events—helped him discover his talent as a porn mogul. With his eyes now opened, he gives his speech:

> Moral fiber. So what is moral fiber? I mean, it's funny. I used to think it was always telling the truth, doing good deeds . . . you know, basically being a f***ing Boy Scout. [The audience gasps.] But lately I've been seeing it differently. Now I think that moral fiber is about finding that one thing you really care about.

That one special thing that means more to you than anything else in the world. [That one special thing in this case being the super-hot porn star/neighbor.]

And when you find her, you fight for her. You risk it all. You put her in front of everything . . . your future, your life . . . all of it. And maybe the stuff you do to help her isn't so clean. You know what? It doesn't matter. Because, in your heart, you know that the juice is worth the squeeze.

Capra-esque, no? (You'll be delighted to know that, in the end, young porn-mogul Matthew gets into Georgetown. Which isn't much of a stretch, actually.)

The truth is, it's hard to find a children's cartoon or movie that doesn't tell kids that they need to look inside themselves for moral guidance. Indeed, there's a riot of Rousseauian claptrap out there that says children are born with rightly ordered consciences. And why not? As Mr. Rogers told us, "You are the most important person in the whole wide world and you hardly even know you." Hillary Clinton is even worse. In her book *It Takes a Village*, she claims that some of the best theologians she's ever met have been five-year-olds (which might be true when compared to a certain homicidal Ukrainian priest).

Such saccharine codswallop overturns millennia of moral teaching. It takes the idea that we must apply reason to nature and our consciences in order to discover what is moral and replaces it with the idea that if it feels right, just do it, baby. Which, by the by, is exactly how Lex Luthor sees the world. *Übermensch*-y passion is now everyone's lodestar. Or as Reese Witherspoon says in *Legally Blonde* 2, "On our very first day at Harvard, a very wise professor quoted Aristotle: 'The law is reason free from passion.' Well, no offense to Aristotle, but in my three years at Harvard I have come to find that passion is a key ingredient to the study and practice of law—and of life."

Well that solves that. Nietzsche-Witherspoon 1, Aristotle 0.

According to Nietzsche's *Zarathustra*, the death of God and the coming of the *übermensch* was going to require the new kind of inner-directed hero to become his own god. As a result, anything society did to inconvenience the heroic individual was morally suspect, a backdoor attempt by The Man to impose conformity. This is pretty much exactly what Robin Williams teaches in *Dead Poets Society*. But that ethos has traveled a long way from Mork. When Barack Obama was asked by a minister to define "sin," he confidently answered that "sin" just means being "out of alignment with my values." Taken literally, this would mean that Hannibal Lecter is being sinful when he abstains from human flesh in favor of a Waldorf salad. As you can see, when you take the modern definition of integrity all the way to the horizon, suddenly "integrity" can only be understood as a firm commitment to one's own principles—because one's own principles are the only legitimate principles. Heck, if you are a god, then doing what you want is God's will.

How's this new morality going to work out for us all? I'm reminded of the time when some entrepreneur announced he was going to release a new line of beer laced with Viagra. Some wag immediately quipped, "What could possibly go wrong?" Which is pretty much where we are today. It's impossible to predict what Integrity 2.0 will yield—because no society in the history of Western civilization has so energetically and deliberately torn down its classical ideal and replaced it with do-it-yourself morality. But a betting man would probably wager that this won't end well.

I suspect that before long we'll be pining for the good old days, when, no matter how often people failed to uphold the standards of integrity, those standards actually meant something.

CHAPTER 16

Curiosity

Maybe the Cat Got What It Had Coming

Christopher Caldwell

A FEW YEARS AGO I was on a British radio show that featured a panel of authors describing their new books. I was having a hard time making the case for mine in the fifteen-second turns we were allotted. A fellow panelist—let's call him Nigel—had no such trouble. Asked by the host what relevance his book might have to current debates, he replied, "Well, Brian, a better question might be: What article of Princess Diana's underclothing was Harrod's magnate Dodi Fayed clutching in his teeth when their Mercedes W140 exploded in a fiery wreck in the Pont de l'Alma tunnel after a night of love and champagne at the Paris Ritz?" He gave no answer. For that you'd have to buy his book. As I recall, plenty of people did.

Nigel understood that curiosity is mighty. It is mightier than arguments. But it is, like many mighty things, hard to define. Curiosity has been little studied by men of science. Psychologists still squabble over whether to think of it as a *trait* (an inborn yearning for knowledge) or a *state* (a kind of discomfort or itch provoked by some specific mystery or temptation). Moralists have been similarly ambivalent. "The gratification of curiosity rather frees us from uneasiness than confers pleasure," said Samuel Johnson. His contemporary Edmund Burke praised curiosity, but only faintly, calling it "the first and simplest emotion we discover in the human mind" and "the most superficial of all the affections." It is hard to say what kind of virtue curiosity is, if indeed it *is* a virtue at all.

It certainly feels like one. Curiosity is associated with a lot of attributes we consider evidence of right living. One is hope, for which "curiosity is little more than another name," as the nineteenth-century English theological writers Augustus and Julius Hare wrote. That students are more eager to learn when they are hopeful, happy, and forward-looking has been agreed upon by pedagogues since the days of Rousseau, who wrote in *Emile*, "There is an ardor to know which is founded only on the desire to be esteemed as learned; there is another ardor which is born of a curiosity natural to man concerning all that might have a connection, close or distant, with his interests."

The problem is that curiosity is associated with hope even when it's leading us into disaster. The cat that curiosity killed was filled with hope, too.

My father worked as a designer of packaging; he was distinguished in his field, and it fascinated him. In connection with his work, he was always designing novelties in his own department, acquiring others at seminars and trade shows, and bringing them home to show his delighted children: six-sided lightbulb boxes, "brick packs" (juice boxes into which you could stab a straw), ingenious blister-wrap-and-cardboard packages. But one winter night in the 1970s he brought home a truly history-changing object—one of the first plastic soft-drink bottles. I think it was a half-gallon bottle of Coca-Cola. My mother and sisters were out when he came up the steps and showed it to me, and he clearly couldn't wait until the whole family saw it. He was right to be giddy. This was really a revolution. The centuries-long age of broken glass bottles was drawing to a close. My father went down the hall to change out of his work clothes, leaving me alone in the living room. Not quite alone, though, because I had my curiosity with me.

The bottle was sitting on the coffee table. I studied it. It occurred to me this thing probably wouldn't break even if you dropped it. I picked the bottle up by its cap, lowered it to six inches off the living-room floor and let it go. *Plunk!* Nothing happened. Amazing. Now I wanted to see just how amazing. I picked the bottle up and held it a foot off the floor. The *plunk!* was a bit louder, loud enough to elicit an "Everything all right out there?" from my father down the hall. The Coke frothed quite a lot. Still . . . it was astonishing. An unbreakable soft-drink bottle! Then I dropped the bottle from two feet.

I probably don't have to describe to you the almost deafening explosion it made as my father emerged into the living room. It drenched the two of us and ruined a rug, a newly upholstered chair, and a set of drapes. Princess Diana's fiery wreck in the Pont de l'Alma tunnel was neither more immediate nor more incendiary than the rage my father flew into. I consoled myself, as I toweled off the wallpaper, that it had been a triumph for the scientific method.

The contemporary psychologists Todd Kashdan and Paul J. Silvia are struck by the fact that curiosity's power can be independent of whether it flatters or gratifies the curious person. "People are often interested in unpleasant, unfamiliar, and possibly unrewarding activities," they write. So while curiosity is related to hope, it should also overlap with humility. A hipster in the habit of eating hummus, jicama, and quinoa can make the experience of eating bad macaroni and cheese tolerable if he can summon the resources of curiosity. While this is a psychological observation, it has much in common with the old religious injunction made to Irish Catholics that, when confronted with a painful or boring thing, they "offer it up"—that is, to endure it bravely in the optimistic spirit that no suffering is without its purpose.

At its extreme, this impulse to treat adversity as something to be learned from is a form of courage—the master virtue, the one without which no other virtue can gain any purchase. Around the time of the Falklands War, I had two friends who were young officers in the Royal Welch Fusiliers. One, whom we'll call Charlie, was preoccupied with what preoccupies most officers—the ability to get one's men to follow one into battle—and made a study of the question. He is now in the British army's top echelons. My other friend, Gareth, took a different approach. His virtues were of the sociable, disorganized kind that are better appreciated in civilian than in military life—getting drunk before work, for instance. I asked Charlie whether Gareth's men would follow him into battle. He paused before saying, "Oh, yes . . . They'd be very curious."

William McDougall, the Harvard professor of psychology who towered over the discipline at the turn of the twentieth century, noted a strong association between curiosity and wonder. In *An Introduction to Social Psychology*, McDougall identified curiosity as the distinctive mark of Western culture. He spoke of the "insatiable curiosity of the modern European and American mind that, more than anything else, distinguishes it from all others," and mentioned wonder "as the name for the primary emotion that accompanies this impulse." Perhaps because McDougall put this message forward as part of a defense of eugenics, his work has mostly been forgotten by historians.

But his thoughts on curiosity were profound and merit revisiting. He believed that civilizational progress was made possible only by the "coexistence and conjoint operation" of conservative religion and progressive science. A civilization lacking one or the other cannot stand, he thought. Just after the First World War he wrote, "At the present time it may seem that in one small quarter of the world, namely, Western Europe, society has achieved an organization so intrinsically stable that it may with impunity tolerate the flourishing of the spirit of inquiry and give free rein to the impulse of curiosity. But to assume that this is the case would be rash." The sentiment is not as obscurantist as it sounds. For McDougall, it was curiosity that spurred both the scientific spirit of inquiry and the religious impulse toward reverence—and curiosity was indispensable to keeping the two in healthy balance.

Curiosity is a protean disposition. The editor Louis Kronenberger, in his memoir of a half-century as publisher, journalist, and author, remembered as one of the highlights of his career a delightful sentence he had discovered in an early draft of Charles Wertenbaker's 1928 novel *Boojum!*: "He went into a restaurant and ordered twenty dollars' worth of scrambled eggs, just to see what they looked like." Here is curiosity at its most ambivalent. Wertenbaker's character is indulging the silliest kind of curiosity, the kind that often comes accompanied with the adjective "idle." But at the same time, Wertenbaker's attempt to *capture* it is evidence of the highest kind of curiosity, the kind that plays the same role in culture that the profit motive does in economics. It is the driving impulse of most of literature, the stuff out of which to build a noble, honorable, and virtuous life.

There are many kinds of curiosity. Only one of them qualifies beyond any shadow of doubt as a virtue: that is intellectual curiosity, or inquisitiveness. By figuring out what we are doing in this world we can come closer to figuring out our purpose in it. Hope and humility combine to make faith—a faith that, once a commitment to discovery is made, life will yield up sense. Saint Paul believes this, writing in 1 Corinthians: "God is faithful, who will not suffer you to be tempted above that ye are able; but will with the temptation also make a way to escape, that ye may be able to bear it."

But it is not a purely religious thought, for Karl Marx thinks a version of it just as fervently, promising, in his *Contribution to the Critique of Political Economy*, that "mankind always takes up only such problems as it can solve. . . . We will always find that the problem itself arises only when the material conditions for its solution already exist or are at least in the process of formation." Curiosity is a virtue because the knowledge acquired through curiosity grounds your other virtues, while leaving to you the choice of what those virtues will be.

The problem comes when we ask what knowledge is. Knowing the first canto of Dante's *Inferno* by heart is knowledge. So is knowing that your neighbor's daughter has a bun in the oven. Most people prefer the latter kind of information to the former. They are like Noel Coward in "I've Been to a Marvellous Party":

> You know, if you have any mind a-tall,
> Gibbon's *divine* Decline and Fall—
> Well, it sounds pretty flimsy,
> No more than a whimsy! . . .
> By way of contrast,
> On Wednesday last,
> I went to a *mar*-vellous party.

Or Lord Byron in *Don Juan:*

> Don José and his lady quarrell'd—*why*
> Not any of the many could divine,
> Though several thousand people chose to try
> 'Twas surely no concern of theirs nor mine;
> I loathe that low vice—curiosity;
> But if there's anything in which I shine,

'Tis in arranging all my friends' affairs.
Not having, of my own, domestic cares.

In the popular mind, curiosity is less often associated with scholarship than with its ne'er-do-well siblings: gossip and prurience. The economist and psychologist George Loewenstein has written of "curiosity's peculiar combination of *superficiality* and *intensity*." In the older Western tradition this combination is a womanly one, as Loewenstein notes, and our literature is full of women whose desire to get to the bottom of things leads to disaster—running from Pandora through Eve to Lot's wife and, eventually, *I Love Lucy*. Counterproductive nosiness is, however, a failing that afflicts all human beings. In his *Confessions*, Augustine writes of this inability to leave well enough alone, describing the retort of a Christian he knew who was being harassed by a questioner about what God had done before he created Heaven and Earth. Augustine quotes the man as having replied, "*Scrutantibus gehennas parabat.*" (He was getting hell ready for busybodies).

When people speak of "low" curiosity, they often mean gossip, but it can describe almost any kind of novelty-seeking. In a modern society built around the marketing of sensations, hedonism has increasingly laid claim to the status of . . . well, not knowledge, perhaps, but at least a kind of expertise. The line blurs between taste and thought, between connoisseurship and wisdom. A sentence such as *He seemed open-minded but he wouldn't smoke marijuana with us* would be unintelligible to John Stuart Mill. Yet such sentiments don't sound so odd today. It might not be considered an abuse of the word "curious" to say you're "curious" about whether Old Overholt makes you drunker than Jim Beam or whether the videos on one pornographic website are better than the ones on another. Again, such a use of "curious" might have been odd a hundred years ago, but it hasn't been since the release, in 1968, of *I Am Curious (Yellow)*—the only X-rated film to feature both Martin Luther King and assassinated Swedish prime minister Olof Palme. (Not that I'm trying to make you curious.)

There really is a hedonistic element in curiosity, in that satisfying one's drive toward it can be a liberation or—if not handled responsibly—an enslavement. Today's online companies understand curiosity's compulsive power. Consider the preposterous headlines that AOL runs over what used to be a "news" site. Instead of enlightening the reader, AOL abuses him—rather than impart information, it alerts him to his deficiencies. So on Groundhog Day, when other websites pointed out that a Pennsylvania groundhog had seen his shadow, betokening six more weeks of winter, AOL headlined, "What did Punxsutawney Phil predict?"

You can tell a lot about a culture by which kinds of curiosity it fosters and which it represses. In earlier times, parents dissuaded children from idle curiosity with fairy tales, but told them to "stop, look, and listen" when it came to important matters. Today, idle curiosity, the kind that leads to clicks, hits, and tweets, is encouraged while barriers are erected to constructive curiosity. Consider the case of the pyramid schemer Bernard Madoff: His impossibly high returns drew notice from financial analysts as early as the 1990s, but financial watchdogs were dissuaded from investigating him by the real risk they would be sued.

If we consider "virtue" the name for a weakness that can be used by the worldly against those who possess it, then curiosity is certainly a virtue. In a world of "big data," built on the tracking and inventorying of individual Internet users' behavior, curiosity is guilelessness. The curious person reveals himself to marketers and the other authorities who shape his life and shows them he has "nothing to hide." The virtuous citizen is one who follows his impulses wherever his own ambition or other people's advertisements lead him. This is an inversion of traditional moral practices. "Curiosity" is a virtue in much the way that "boldness" or "insubordination" is. It is vitally important in some times and contexts. It is an outright vice in others.

CHAPTER 17

Perseverance

All the Way to the End

Christopher Buckley

PERSEVERANCE ISN'T A WORD you hear much today. It doesn't roll trippingly off the modern American tongue. At four syllables, it takes perseverance just to pronounce it. A quaint, biblical word, a relic preserved under glass or in aspic, or embroidered a century and a half ago by a New England schoolgirl named, say, Abigail, on a piece of muslin. I cannot recall when I last heard it aloud.

But as a concept, perseverance rocks. It rules. Its antonym, giving up or quitting, is regarded as odious and—worse—un-American. Quitting has been the subject of spluttering excoriations by such paragons of see-the-thing-throughness and victory-at-all-costs as Theodore Roosevelt, General Patton, Vince Lombardi, Bluto Blutarsky, and a thousand self-help gurus. *Pick yourself up, dust yourself off! You can* do *it!*

Of all the "deadly" virtues extolled in this attractively packaged and reasonably priced little volume, perseverance may be the one that most lends itself to motto, sloganeering, and escutcheon. You could do worse than have on your coat of arms the concise boast: *Persevero.* I persevere.

In heraldry, this virtue is traditionally represented by three symbols: the beaver, the camel, and the snail. Not quite totems to strike fear into a black knight charging at you on his steed, twirling a nail-studded battle mace. But these gentle creatures do embody reliability and durability.

Beaver dams attest to the implacable industry of these erst-while suppliers of hat-making material. Pre–Range Rovers, the camel got the job done. One thinks of the scene in *Lawrence of Arabia* as Lawrence and Sharif Ali stare out over the vast furnace of the Nefud Desert, which must be crossed to attack the Turkish garrison at Aqaba. Ali remarks with Bedouin sangfroid: "If the camels die, we die. And in twenty days they will start to die." (In reality, Lawrence and his men never actually crossed the Nefud on the way to Aqaba; they skirted its edge. But why tamper with a great line?)

As for the humble but determined snail, the influential Victorian preacher Charles Spurgeon paid it this high accolade: "By perseverance the snail reached the ark." I prefer another gloss on the indomitability of the noble mollusk: A man lives alone in the middle of the forest. One night he hears a knock on the door. Opens it, no one's there. As he closes the door, he sees a snail on the stoop. He picks it up and hurls it with force back into the forest. Three months later, he hears another knock on the door. Opens it. Snail says, "Whadja do *that* for?"

But then, we don't use coats of arms much anymore. Today, we proclaim our personal slogans and mantras on bumper stickers and refrigerator magnets. One of the most prominent of the latter variety is a distinctive, white-on-red poster of British World War II vintage urging—commanding—the viewer to KEEP CALM AND CARRY ON. If you thought, as I did, that this was a slogan to sustain Londoners through the Blitz, you would be incorrect. No, this particular poster was never actually deployed. It had been prepared in the event of an invasion. Thanks mainly to the valor of the Royal Air Force, it was never needed. The threat of German invasion is now, happily, a very distant prospect for Britons and Americans, and yet the slogan adorns Frigidaires and Sub-Zeros everywhere.

Are things *that* bad? Or does this indicate that we have a primal need to be bucked up and encouraged not to throw in the towel? KEEP CALM AND CARRY ON is a dignified exhortation, quintessentially British, especially compared with its modern, American variations, which include "Keep on Truckin'" and "Keep On Keepin' On." It certainly beats the fatalistic millennial *cri de coeur*, "Suck It Up, Bitch."

Another P-themed refrigerator magnet much on view these days is, "Never, never, never, never give in!" That's a bit strident, but then we're a culture whose idea of persevering is "Thank God It's Friday"—*Wow, we made it all the way to Friday!*

The author of "never, never, never" is, of course, that archetypal bulldog of pluck, indomitability, and Vitamin P—Winston Churchill. It's from a speech he gave in October 1941 to the students at Harrow School, boys who soon would be shouldering the burden of battle themselves. His actual words were, "Never give in, never give in, *never, never, never, never*—in nothing, great or small, large or petty—never give in except to convictions of honour and good sense."

Churchill's rhetoric was at its most stirring when the chips were down, when perseverance was an even more indispensable quality than courage. He gave four speeches during the war with perseverance as the centerpiece: "Blood, toil, tears, and sweat"; "We shall fight on the beaches"; the Harrow speech; and this one, arguably the most moving, after the fall of France, when things were darkest:

> Let us therefore brace ourselves to our duties, and
> so bear ourselves, that if the British Empire and its
> Commonwealth last for a thousand years, men will
> still say, "This was their finest hour."

That "thousand" was not a random number. Hitler had declared a "thousand-year Reich." This was to be a contest to see whose system would persevere over the other.

Churchill could also be rather witty on the subject, as he was when he said, "If you are going through hell, keep going." But my favorite is his private mantra on that theme, condensed to a three-letter acronym: "KBO." It's scrawled on a coffee-stained, weathered Post-It note on my desk. It stands for "Keep Buggering On." It works for me, but if you're going to declaim it out loud at the dinner table, discretion is probably advised.

Churchill was the product of an age—the Victorian—that exalted perseverance above other virtues for reasons both spiritual and practical. It was a jolly admirable quality in and of itself, but there was also a monarchy to sustain against mounting republican sentiment, uppity colonies full of mutinous wogs, and other formidable empires to fight. For Rudyard Kipling, the era's most lapidary spokesman, perseverance served as the theme for his best-remembered poem:

> If you can force your heart and nerve and sinew
> To serve your turn long after they are gone,
> And so hold on when there is nothing in you
> Except the Will which says to them: "Hold on!"

Another English poet of the time, William Earnest Henley (note the middle name), made it the subject of his signature piece, "Invictus": "My head is bloody, but unbowed. . . . I am the master of my fate / I am the captain of my soul." It was Tennyson in 1842 who first enshrined perseverance as a particularly Victorian virtue: "Come, my friends, / 'Tis not too late to seek a newer world . . . / To strive, to seek, to find, and not to yield." It's the motto of Outward Bound. To this day *Ulysses* surely remains the quintessential inspirational poem.

In America, at about the time Tennyson was sharpening his quills, a rhyme was introduced to schoolchildren. It survives today, amid the militant emphasis on diversity, differently abled–ness, gender neutrality, and other contemporary virtues. It went—rather, it goes—like this:

> If you find your task is hard,
> Try, try again
> Time will bring you your reward
> Try, try again
> All that other folks can do
> Why, with patience, should not you?
> Only keep this rule in view
> Try, try again.

It's from *The McGuffey Reader*. Some 120 million copies of it were placed in the grubby little hands of American schoolchildren between the 1830s and 1960s. "Try, try again" is a more accessible (as we say today) concept than "perseverance." Same idea, only barefoot and wearing a straw hat, like Huck Finn. An adjunct concept, self-reliance, would soon become a great theme of Emerson and the Transcendentalists, sending Henry David Thoreau off into the woods in a postindustrial revolutionary huff. (How delicious it was to learn that his mother continued to do his laundry while he self-reliantly rusticated on the shores of Walden Pond.)

As I type, today's *New York Times* brings the obituary of a Brigadier General Robinson Risner. He was shot down over Vietnam in 1965 and endured one of the longest captivities in that misnamed hellhole usually called the "Hanoi Hilton." Among the tortures he suffered were three years' solitary confinement—in total darkness. As the obit recounted, "He once experienced an anxiety attack, but knew he would be beaten if he screamed. He stuffed a blanket in his mouth." Civilian perseverance is a fine thing; in a warrior, noble.

Laura Hillenbrand has built a brilliant literary career on the theme of perseverance, most recently with her account of the ordeal of Louie Zamperini. Zamperini was Job on steroids. After his plane ditched in the Pacific, he spent forty-seven days adrift in a raft croaking from thirst, scorched by the sun, and snapped at by ravening sharks. Having somehow survived that, he washed up on a beach into a notoriously sadistic Japanese prison camp. Having survived *that*, he returned home to drink and to the nightmares of posttrauma. But in the end he emerges, as the book's title asserts, unbroken.

It is staggering and humbling to contemplate what soldiers endure: the winter of 1778 at Valley Forge, the suicide assaults on Marye's Heights at Fredericksburg, the phosgene gas–choked trenches of World War I. Inside the German gun emplacement at Pointe du Hoc in Normandy is a plaque that commemorates what Lieutenant Colonel Rudder and his Rangers managed on that June day in 1944. It includes his bewildered remark to his son when they visited the site ten years later: "Will you tell me how we did this?" As James Michener wrote at the end of his Korean War saga, *The Bridges of Toko-Ri*, "Where do we find such men?"

But then, where do we find such women as Laura Hillenbrand, who wrote *Unbroken* and *Seabiscuit*—a triumphant account of equine perseverance—while so crippled by chronic fatigue syndrome that she was unable to leave her apartment? Or Flannery O'Connor, who, while dying of lupus, forced herself to stay awake at the typewriter by immersing her feet in buckets of ice water. Ulysses S. Grant raced against throat cancer in order to finish the memoir that would support his family. He refused pain medicine so as to keep his mind clear. The most majestic example of writerly perseverance is surely Solzhenitsyn. After years in Stalin's Gulag, he was sent into internal exile with a mortal diagnosis of cancer. Determined to continue documenting the Soviet holocaust, he went on writing, on strips of paper he concealed in a bottle, which he buried to avoid confiscation by the KGB.

Explorers are conspicuous civilian heroes of perseverance. Sir Richard Burton, Dr. Livingstone, John Hanning Speke, Ernest Shackleton—to name just a handful of doughty examples—occupy spacious niches in this pantheon. But explorers, like soldiers, often don't have much choice in the matter: it's persevere or die. Not a lot of choice there. That being the case, does simple endurance amount to perseverance? For that matter, doesn't perseverance, as a virtue, rather depend on the *object* of the quest?

When former president Theodore Roosevelt embarked on his daring expedition down the "River of Doubt" in South America, he was seeking to advance human knowledge. But consider, then, other explorers of that general region, the *conquistadores* of sixteenth-century Imperial Spain. These armored bravos certainly persevered amid formidable obstacles. But their quest (for gold, slaves, colonies, converts to the One and True Faith) could hardly be called disinterested, much less glorious. Among the terrors that Roosevelt and his people had to contend with as they made their way through a thousand miles of steaming, pestilential tropical soup was a variety of toothpick-sized catfish called the *candiru* that swim up the urethra and . . . well . . . *lodge* there. Reading William Prescott's *Conquest of Mexico and Peru* is apt to make the reader wish *candiru* up the urinary tracts of these rapacious, sanguinary Spanish *capitans* so that they won't persevere.

On a larger scale, can it be said that evil perseveres? Or does it merely perdure? Did the Soviet Union "persevere" for those seventy-four long years? Or just last? North Korea is now ruled by a third generation of the grotesque Kim dynasty. Fidel Castro is in his sixth decade in office, having outlasted (persevered?) everything the mightiest nation on earth threw at him: the Bay of Pigs, a naval blockade, the U.S. embargo, and multiple Katzenjammer CIA assassination schemes. "'Tis known by the name of perseverance in a good cause," as Tristam Shandy said, "and of obstinacy in a bad one."

And so we come to the knotty question: Is perseverance—in a good cause, that is—*necessarily* a virtue?

Ten years after JFK put the phrase "long twilight struggle" into circulation, a disillusioned young veteran went before the Senate and demanded, "How do you ask a man to be the last man to die in Vietnam? How do you ask a man to be the last man to die for a mistake?" As Vietnam devolved into quagmire, our government was at pains to reassure us that there was "light at the end of the tunnel." This figure of speech became, first, problematic, then risible. It was code for, "Yeah, right."

Neil Sheehan's epic account of the U.S. experience in Vietnam, *A Bright Shining Lie*, contains an indelible, tragicomic vignette. It is 1967. John Paul Vann, the American most knowledgeable about Vietnam, has been sent back there by the Pentagon to evaluate the situation. He learns that the situation is pretty damn well hopeless, and he returns to Washington to deliver this news that no one wants to hear. He's summoned to the White House to brief National Security Advisor Walt Rostow. Rostow listens to Vann's gloomy report until he can no longer bear any more. He begins to fidget with desk papers. Finally he interrupts Vann to ask if—*surely*—the United States will be over the worst of the war in six months? Vann tells him, "Oh hell no, Mr. Rostow. I'm a born optimist. I think we can hold out longer than that."

Behavioral scientists speak of something called a "sunk cost fallacy." Once you've invested time and money in something—war, a new product, trying to find the South Pole—you're prone to keep at it even when doing so no longer makes much rational sense. Yet on the other hand, American business books extol entrepreneurs who kept going when everyone around them said to give up. Even so, there are occasions when, really, it would have made more sense to fold the cards. Mark Twain found this out the very hard way when he persisted in pouring his fortune—and his wife's—into the Paige Compositor. Had it worked, it would have revolutionized newspaper typesetting. But it didn't work, and Twain was ruined.

Ernest Shackleton is greatly hailed today for his astonishing feat of perseverance after his ship *Endurance* came to grief during his Antarctic expedition in 1914. But he should also be esteemed for his pre-*Endurance* expedition, when he decided to turn back from the South Pole, less than one hundred miles from his goal. That decision has been described as one of the most admirable—and toughest—decisions ever made in the field of exploration. He could have been the first one to get to the South Pole, but as tempted as he was to go for the glory, he realized they'd never make it to base camp. As it was, they barely made it, and he had to rely on "forced march" pills—cocaine—to survive. On the way home from Antarctica, he explained his decision in a telegram to his wife: "I thought you would prefer a live donkey to a dead lion."

A couple years later, explorer Robert Scott killed himself and three others with perseverance. While Amundsen was easily skiing and dog-sledding to the Pole—and gaining weight on the trip!—Scott insisted on having his guys man-haul the sleds, and insisted on weighing them down with rocks collected for scientific purposes. They lugged those rocks to the very end. Ironically, the disaster made Scott a national hero. But then, the Brits have always been infatuated with glorious failures.

A surviving member of the Scott expedition, Apsley Cherry-

Garrard, went on to write *The Worst Journey in the World*, in which he offered this somewhat unfashionable assessment of the British performance:

> I now see very plainly that though we achieved a first-rate tragedy, which will never be forgotten just because it was a tragedy, tragedy was not our business. In the broad perspective opened up by ten years' distance, I see not one journey to the Pole, but two, in startling contrast one to another. On the one hand, Amundsen going straight there, getting there first, and returning without the loss of a single man, and without having put any greater strain on himself and his men than was all in the day's work of polar exploration. Nothing more business-like could be imagined. On the other hand, our expedition, running appalling risks, performing prodigies of super-human endurance, achieving immortal renown, commemorated in august cathedral sermons and by public statues, yet reaching the Pole only to find our terrible journey superfluous, and leaving our best men dead on the ice. To ignore such a contrast would be ridiculous: to write a book without accounting for it a waste of time.

That line—"Tragedy was not our business"—has been widely cited. It could be engraved as a footnote on all those monuments to Scott and the men he sacrificed.

Without perseverance, nothing is accomplished. But blind perseverance can lead to tragedy, when tragedy was never the object. Perseverance must march hand-in-hand with her sister virtues. When she does, she is majestic indeed.

Author Bios

CHRISTOPHER BUCKLEY is an American political satirist and the author of novels including *God Is My Broker, Thank You for Smoking, Little Green Men, The White House Mess, No Way to Treat a First Lady, Wet Work, Florence of Arabia, Boomsday, Supreme Courtship, Losing Mum and Pup: A Memoir*, and, most recently, *But Enough about You*. He was chief speechwriter for George H. W. Bush during his vice presidency and was founder and editor-in-chief of *Forbes Life* magazine. He is the recipient of the 2002 Washington Irving Medal for Literary Excellence. In 2004 he was awarded the Thurber Prize for American Humor.

SONNY BUNCH is managing editor of the *Washington Free Beacon*. Prior to joining the *Beacon*, he served as a staff writer at the *Washington Times*, an assistant editor at the *Weekly Standard*, and an editorial assistant at *Roll Call*. Bunch's work has appeared in the *Wall Street Journal, Commentary, Reason*, the *New Atlantis, Policy Review*, and elsewhere. A 2004 graduate of the University of Virginia, Bunch lives in Alexandria, Virginia.

DAVID BURGE is a hobbyist writer and hot rodder who blogs and tweets as Iowahawk (@iowahawkblog). He is a frequent contributor to *Garage Magazine*, and his articles have appeared in the *Weekly Standard, Middle East Quarterly*, the *European Business Journal*, and *Readings in American Government*. Native to Chicago, he remains, despite his better judgment, a committed Cubs fan.

CHRISTOPHER CALDWELL is a senior editor at the *Weekly Standard* and a columnist for the *Financial Times*. He is the author of *Reflections on the Revolution in Europe: Immigration, Islam, and the West.*

ANDREW FERGUSON is senior editor at the *Weekly Standard*. Before joining the *Standard* at its founding in 1995, he was a senior writer at the *Washingtonian* magazine, He has been a columnist for *Fortune*, Bloomberg News, *TV Guide*, *Commentary*, and *Forbes FYI* and a contributing editor to *Time* magazine. He is the author of *Fools' Names, Fools' Faces*; *Land of Lincoln*; and *Crazy U.*

JONAH GOLDBERG is a syndicated columnist and author. Goldberg is known for his contributions on politics and culture to *National Review Online*, of which he is editor-at-large. He is the author of *Liberal Fascism* (2008), a number-one *New York Times* best seller, and most recently, *The Tyranny of Clichés*, also a national best seller. He was the founding editor of National Review Online and is a fellow at the American Enterprise Institute. He is a regular columnist for *USA Today* and the *Los Angeles Times* and is a Fox News Contributor (and frequent member of the Special Report "All Star" panel). He was ranked as one of the *Atlantic* magazine's fifty most influential commentators in America. He also watches too much TV.

MICHAEL GRAHAM is a talk radio host, political commentator, former GOP political consultant, and sometime stand-up comedian. He proudly notes that he must be the only person on earth to open for Bill Maher, Chris Rock, and Sarah Palin.

Graham's radio career has taken him up the East Coast from Charleston to Washington, before spending time in Boston and, most recently, Atlanta. The author of four books, including the first major-published book on the Tea Party movement—*That's No Angry Mob, That's My Mom!*—Graham is also a regular Monday guest on NewsTalk's *The Right Hook* with George Hook in Ireland.

MOLLIE HEMINGWAY is a senior editor at the *Federalist*. She was previously a columnist for *Christianity Today* and contributor to GetReligion.org. Her writing on religion, economics, and baseball has appeared in the *Wall Street Journal*, the *Los Angeles Times*, the *Guardian, Federal Times, Radio & Records*, and *Modern Reformation*. Originally from Colorado, she lives in Washington with her husband and two children. She enjoys combing flea markets to improve her vinyl record collection and believes that the designated hitter rule is the result of a communist plot.

RITA KOGANZON is a graduate student in government at Harvard University. She has written for the *New Atlantis, Policy Review, National Affairs*, and other publications.

MATT LABASH is a senior writer at the *Weekly Standard*. His collection *Fly Fishing with Darth Vader: And Other Adventures with Evangelical Wrestlers, Political Hitmen, and Jewish Cowboys* was published in 2010 by Simon and Schuster. He lives in Owings, Maryland.

JONATHAN V. LAST is a senior writer at the *Weekly Standard* and author of *What to Expect When No One's Expecting: America's Coming Demographic Disaster*. His writings have been featured in the *Wall Street Journal*, the *Washington Post*, the *Claremont Review of Books, First Things*, and elsewhere.

JAMES LILEKS is a columnist for the *Minneapolis Star-Tribune,* a columnist for *National Review,* and author of *Tiny Lies, Falling up the Stairs,* and *Graveyard Special.* He has lived in Minneapolis since 1976, with a four-year tour of duty in Washington, DC. He hosted talk radio in the 1980s and '90s, and curates a number of blogs and websites, including the Institute of Official Cheer, home of the infamous *Gallery of Regrettable Food.*

ROB LONG is a writer and television producer in Hollywood, California. As a writer and coexecutive producer for the long-running television program *Cheers,* he received Emmy and Golden Globe nominations in 1992 and 1993. He went on to have a string of cancelled television series. His current uncancelled series, *Sullivan & Son,* airs on TBS. In addition to his television work, Long is a contributing editor for *National Review* and a weekly columnist for the English-language Abu Dhabi daily, the *National.* His weekly public radio commentary, *Martini Shot,* is broadcast nationally and on KCRW.com. His two books, *Conversations with My Agent* and *Set Up, Joke, Set Up, Joke* were recently reissued by Bloomsbury. In May 2010 he cofounded a new center-right commentary site, *Ricochet.*

LARRY MILLER is an actor, comedian, voice artist, podcaster, and columnist. He has appeared in over one hundred film and television shows, including *Seinfeld* and *10 Things I Hate about You,* as well as several characters in Christopher Guest's mockumentary films. His other credits include *Pretty Woman, The Nutty Professor, Nutty Professor II: The Klumps, Law & Order,* and *Boston Legal.* In addition, he's a contributing humorist to the *Huffington Post* and the *Weekly Standard,* as well as the author of the best-selling book, *Spoiled Rotten America.* Miller hosts the podcast *This Week with Larry Miller* on Carolla Digital, where he unleashes a barrage of humor about the absurdities of daily life.

P. J. O'ROURKE is an American political satirist, journalist, and author. O'Rourke is the H. L. Mencken Research Fellow at the Cato Institute, writes a weekly column for the *Daily Beast*, is a regular correspondent for the *Weekly Standard*, and is a frequent panelist on National Public Radio's game show *Wait Wait . . . Don't Tell Me!* He is the author of seventeen books, including the *New York Times* best sellers *Parliament of Whores* and *Give War a Chance*. His latest book, *The Baby Boom: How It Got That Way . . . And It Wasn't My Fault . . . And I'll Never Do It Again*, was released in January 2014. According to a *60 Minutes* profile, he is also the most quoted living man in *The Penguin Dictionary of Modern Humorous Quotations*.

JOE QUEENAN writes the "Moving Targets" column for the *Wall Street Journal*. Author of nine books, his work has appeared in *Time, Newsweek, Rolling Stone, GQ, Forbes, Spy*, the *New York Times Book Review*, the *Los Angeles Times*, and the *Guardian*. His memoir, *Closing Time*, appeared on the *New York Times* list of 100 Notable Books of 2009. A native of Philadelphia, he now lives in Tarrytown, New York.

CHRISTINE ROSEN is senior editor of the *New Atlantis: A Journal of Technology & Society*, where she writes about the social impact of technology, bioethics, and the history of genetics. She is the author of *Preaching Eugenics: Religious Leaders and the American Eugenics Movement* and *My Fundamentalist Education*. Since 1999 Ms. Rosen has also been an adjunct scholar at the American Enterprise Institute for Public Policy Research. Her essays and reviews have appeared in publications such as the *New York Times Magazine*, the *Wall Street Journal*, the *New Republic*, the *Washington Post*, the *American Historical Review*, the *Weekly Standard, Commentary*, and the *New England Journal of Medicine*.

ANDREW STILES is the digital managing editor for the *Washington Free Beacon* and a contributor to the Editor's Blog, where he specializes in political and cultural analysis. His work has been featured in the *Washington Post* and denounced in countless other publications. Previously, he covered Congress as a reporter for *National Review*. He lives in Washington, DC.